I ♥ My Dog!

I ♥ My Dog!

The All-Around Guide to Choosing, Training, Grooming and Caring for Your Best Friend

WITH PHOTOGRAPHS BY LAURA MOSS

Woman's Day

Copyright © 2010 Filipacchi Publishing,
a division of Hachette Filipacchi Media
U.S., Inc.

Photographs © 2010 Laura Moss

First published in 2010 in the United States
of America by
Filipacchi Publishing
1633 Broadway
New York, NY 10019

Woman's Day is a registered trademark of
Hachette Filipacchi Media U.S., Inc.

ISBN-13: 978-1-933231-72-3

Library of Congress Control Number:
2009938284

Design: Patricia Fabricant
Editor: Lauren Kuczala
Production: Lynn Scaglione

Printed in China

You want a friend for life?
Get a dog.

Harry Truman

Dogs are our link to paradise.
They don't know evil or jealousy
or discontent.

Milan Kundera

CONTENTS

CHOOSING *the* RIGHT DOG *for* YOU

Dog ownership is a serious commitment. While it's easy to fall head over heels for an adorable puppy, the wise individual or family will do their homework before taking this momentous step. First and foremost, try to honestly evaluate whether you have sufficient time, energy and resources to devote to a new family member—since a dog requires nearly the same amount of care. Also make sure to thoroughly research the breed of dog you're interested in. Then assess your family's "profile" to determine if that breed will be the best fit with your habits and lifestyle. Taking the time to answer a few key questions can save a lot of trouble, expense and even heartache down the road.

9

All About Dogs

There are a number of interesting animal facts you may not know about your four-legged friend.

1 **Did you know that a dog's only sweat glands are on his footpads?** A dog's primary method of cooling off is through panting, making dogs less efficient at keeping cool than humans, who have sweat glands all over their bodies.

2 **One of the more interesting animal facts:** A dog's noseprint is just like a human's fingerprints—unique. Just like fingerprints, noseprints can be used to accurately identify the owner of that nose.

3 **Humans have been keeping dogs as pets for more than 12,000 years.** No wonder they are known as "man's best friend"—they are his oldest friend!

4 **The largest dog breed in the world is the Irish wolfhound;** the smallest is the Chihuahua. The Saint Bernard is the heaviest breed of dog.

5 **The basenji, an African wolf dog, is the only dog in the world that cannot bark.** If you're looking for a quiet dog, the basenji would be a good choice.

6 **A dog's sense of smell is over 100,000 times more sensitive than a human's.** The bloodhound is best known for its keen sense of smell and tracking abilities, and is often used by law enforcement.

7 **Puppies sleep a lot.** They actually sleep about 90 percent of the day for their first few weeks.

8 **Dogs have twice as many muscles in their ears as humans.** This is why they are able to move their ears around so well, but people can't.

9 **Dogs have an amazingly keen sense of hearing;** it's their second most developed sense after smell, of course. A dog can detect sound frequencies in the range of 67 Hz to 45 kHz. Humans can detect sound frequencies up to 20 kHz.

10 **Dogs are pack animals.** They are naturally submissive to any person or other canine with a higher pack status. They also quickly and easily recognize this higher pack status in another dog or human. A dog will demonstrate its submission by lying down and presenting its belly to the pack leader.

How to Pick the Perfect Pooch for Your Family

What breed suits your lifestyle best?

Outdoorsy, athletic families often lean toward dogs, while people looking for a lower-maintenance pet tend to choose cats. Relaxed families may prefer laid-back bulldogs, while active families are best for high-energy huskies, retrievers and dalmatians. Only the most attentive types should adopt border collies and sheepdogs. They need lots of mental and physical stimulation. The best dogs for families with young children are golden retrievers, beagles and English bulldogs, but stay away from tiny "toy" dogs if you have tots. While most dogs are highly adaptable, extreme climates and small spaces can make some dogs miserable. High-energy dogs should not live in areas without fenced-in play areas, even if they receive daily walks. Dogs with thick coats may not thrive in very hot areas and may require shaving, at the very least, to remain comfortable.

What age should the dog be?

Having a puppy is like having a child. You have to puppy-proof your house, toilet-train him and wash him all the time. Also, puppies cry at night and always want to be with you. It's a better idea to choose a dog that's at least 6 months old. At that age, they're more likely to be housebroken and comfortable around people. And forget the myth that adult dogs can't bond with new families, or be retrained if they had a previous owner. It's not difficult to teach a dog new tricks—at any age.

How do you gauge the animal's temperament and personality?

Often when you first meet a dog, he's very freaked out. You don't get to see him as he really is. Your best bet is to ask the people who care for him what he's like. Otherwise, you could have him a week before he shows his true colors.

Shelters often ask dogs' former owners to explain why they gave them up. Many also conduct temperament evaluations. It gives you a clear picture of what life with him will be like.

Will it fit in your budget?

It's easy to forget about the cost of dog ownership. Dogs cost upward of $500 annually in food, grooming and vet bills. Think through all the costs before you take the leap. Shop for toys and food, and research the price of physicals, vaccinations, and flea and heartworm treatments with vets. Too often, people just aren't prepared for the financial burden. Also, dogs can incur unexpected medical expenses.

If you decide your family can't afford a dog right now, consider pet-sitting for a friend or serving as a temporary foster family for an animal shelter. That will help you determine if your kids are really ready for their own dog, and will give you time to save up for one.

Who will take care of it?

Kids will swear they'll be walkers, but Mom and Dad are the default caretakers. For best results, assign pet-care chores to kids right off the bat. Often, caring for an animal can help a kid become more responsible and a better time manager.

Where do you get one?

Check animal shelters and rescue groups first. While they have adoption fees, they're still a less expensive option than a pet shop, where the price for a puppy often starts at $200. Many shelters have other animals in addition to dogs and cats. Check *petfinder.com* to see if the type of pet you want is available for adoption in your area.

Guide to Choosing a Dog Breed

There are many factors, such as the size of the dog and how much exercise it requires, that need to be taken into consideration when trying to determine what breed is right for you. It is important to remember that adopting a dog is a life-changing decision, so you will want to explore all of the breed options before selecting the most suitable one for you.

Size

When choosing a dog breed, it is important to think about size. Some people prefer large dogs, while others prefer smaller ones. It is important to think about the amount of space that you have available for the dog before selecting a size that is suitable for your family. A small dog may be a more suitable choice if you have small children. Large dogs are more likely to play rough and may accidentally cause injuries.

Larger dogs are more expensive than smaller dogs. Everything associated with their care is more expensive: food, toys and boarding will all cost 20 to 50 percent more than for a dog that weighs less than 20 pounds.

Hair and grooming

Some people do not mind dogs that shed. Others do not have the time to vacuum once or twice daily. If there is someone in the household who is allergic to pet dander, it may be a good idea to stay away from some of the dogs that have longer hair, such as golden retrievers. There are many dog breeds that do not shed at all, or only shed minimally. Some of the options to take into consideration include poodles, shih tzus and Portuguese water dogs. Mixed breeds such as cockapoos or Labradoodles are known to be a great choice for those with allergies.

While some dogs may only require a bath every six to eight weeks, others will need professional grooming and daily brushing to look good. Poodles, for example, are intelligent dogs that are easily trained, but may require too much grooming for the average pet owner. Calling local grooming shops and asking for grooming fees for different types of dogs can help you refine your budget in these areas.

Health

Health problems may take some owners by surprise, but many diagnoses are common within certain breeds. Genetically, certain breed types are prone to specific injuries and illnesses. Breeds such as boxers often die of cancer, while extra-large breeds can easily injure themselves. No matter what type of dog you have, buying pet health insurance can help you pay for unexpected emergencies.

Trainability

An easily trained dog is essential for first-time dog owners. Dogs that are more difficult to train can frustrate novice owners. Choosing a dog that is eager to please can make training time more pleasant. Also, do not make the mistake of thinking that intelligent dogs will be easy to train. One of the most intelligent breeds, basenjis, are notoriously difficult to train and may never respond consistently to commands.

Energy and exercise

Before selecting a dog, it is important to think about how much exercise the breed requires, as well as how much exercise you are able to give a dog. If you are an athletic or outdoorsy type, a dog that has a lot of energy may be the right choice for you. Some great options include Labrador and golden retrievers, and border collies. If you do not have the time or motivation to constantly exercise your dog, then breeds with lower energy are more ideal. These include the shih tzu, pug and Maltese.

Keep in mind that when selecting a dog breed based on energy levels, it is also important to consider space. If you live in a tiny apartment with no yard, a lower-energy dog is probably the best option. Bored, overactive dogs are a common source of problems for pet owners. A brisk, daily walk of at least 20 minutes is recommended for all breeds. For high-energy breeds, a daily walk of an hour and vigorous play may be required.

Your experience level

Dog ownership is only easy in theory. Some breeds require a lot of specialized care. Therefore, if you are a novice pet owner, you can easily get frustrated with all of your "doggy duties." Keep this in mind and select a dog that fits your level of experience as a pet owner. Get a low-maintenance dog if it's your first time out. Go for a more challenging breed if you are a seasoned and capable dog owner.

Tips for Choosing a Dog for Children

If your child has recently asked for a dog, then chances are you have questions about choosing one to fit your family's needs. You want to find the right breed to interact well with your children, to adapt to your lifestyle and to get along with any other family pets.

Examine the dog's personality

One important aspect in choosing a dog for your children is to evaluate the dog's temperament and personality. Look for dogs that like to be touched and do not mind loud noises. Since children are active, nonstop bundles of energy, you want a dog that can keep up with exuberant behavior and can thrive in this environment. A mixed-breed, young adult dog is a perfect pick for children. These dogs may already be house trained and may have outgrown the problems they experienced during their puppy years. According to the Humane Society of the United States, mixed-breed dogs also are less prone to suffering from genetic defects.

Interview the animal shelter staff

As you view a particular dog at your local shelter, ask the staff about temperament. What have the employees observed? Does the dog bark excessively? Does he growl at people? Read through any history the staff may have on the dog. Bring your children with you during this interview process and watch how the dog interacts with them. You can determine almost immediately if a particular dog is receptive to children or not.

Evaluate your lifestyle

As you evaluate potential dogs for your children, consider your lifestyle. Do your children enjoy walking and hiking? What ages are your children? If you have young children, you may want to consider a dog with boundless energy for playing tag, chase or fetch. If you have teenagers, you may want to look at mature dogs. Mature dogs require less training and do well with gentler playtime. Consider your house and yard. Do you have enough space for a big dog to romp around with your children? Is your yard fenced? How will you keep the dog from running loose? If you have a small yard or no yard at all, then a small, mixed breed may be the best option for your child. A large dog will thrive in big yards and will require daily walks and play sessions.

Consider other family pets

When choosing a dog for your children, you need to consider the other pets in your home. If your child will be taking care of the new dog, decide if your child will also take care of other pets or if you will assume the task. Caring for a new dog takes a considerable amount of time and energy. You want to ensure that existing pets feel safe and secure with a new dog. Before you purchase the dog, observe how he reacts around other dogs or cats. If you have cats, be sure to avoid dog breeds that act aggressively toward small animals.

How to teach children dog-friendly behavior

When dogs bite, kids under 12 are most often the victims. Many nips occur when children run up to unfamiliar dogs that aren't in the mood to play. Kids watch cartoons and see animals as extremely friendly, cuddly, affectionate things. Teach a child early on that a dog is its own being and may not want to be approached.

* **Don't** run up to an unknown dog. First, ask (or have the child ask) the owner if the dog is friendly. If so, walk up to the dog slowly. If the child is very young, stay with him, placing yourself between him and the dog.

* **Don't** be fooled by a wagging tail. It's not always a sign of friendliness. Tell your child that if the dog is barking or backing away while wagging its tail, she should let the pup alone.

* **Do** let the dog take the lead. A child should remain motionless and hold out his hand, softly calling for the dog. If it approaches, he can let the dog sniff his hand. Only then should the child start gentle petting. This sniff-then-pet exchange is a gesture of friendliness, the doggie equivalent of shaking hands.

* **Don't** touch a dog that is sleeping, eating, drinking or chewing on a toy.

16

Top 10 Breeds for Kids

1 Golden retriever Shaggy, friendly and very intelligent, golden retrievers can draw a ray of sunshine over any home with kids. Their predilection toward games and their willingness to fetch will keep your children busy in the backyard for hours while you enjoy some time to yourself. Goldens are also very protective, especially around children.

2 American bulldog These pug-faced pooches might look a bit hostile at first, but they are very gentle at heart. They do require lots of exercise to keep them stimulated, but they build nurturing relationships with kids and tend to be loyal toward their owners.

3 Beagle Small and compact, beagles are one of the most convenient dog breeds for families with children because they are easily transported and don't eat families out of house and home. Although they have a tendency to dig in the yard and bark at passersby, they are also content to lie on the couch with their human family members for hours on end.

4 English shepherd An English shepherd is a calm, obedient, fiercely loyal dog with a desire to protect the family and a strong work ethic. These dogs enjoy having a job, and have recently become very popular with agility events, but integrate well with children as long as they are given plenty of time to run and play.

5 Labrador retriever Very affectionate and drawn toward children, Labrador retrievers are among the most pleasant dog breeds, although they are quite large. Labradors love water and will spend hours playing in the sprinkler with your kids or jumping in the lake to retrieve tennis balls.

6 Newfoundland These are very patient and kind and very intelligent. They are large and furry, which might mean more housekeeping if you want to keep hair on the furniture to a minimum, but they tend to love kids and bask in affection.

7 Saint Bernard What kid wouldn't want his or her own Beethoven? Saint Bernards are enormous, friendly dogs with an easy disposition and an ingrained desire to please. They learn quickly and respond well to multiple commands, though you'll want to watch out for excessive drooling at mealtimes.

8 Springer spaniel Some spaniels are a bit aggressive, but this isn't the case for the springer spaniel. These dogs are sensitive and sometimes slow to warm up to strangers, but they form lifelong bonds with their owners and love to play with kids. Some springers might be a little too needy, however, so make sure to encourage independence.

9 Havanese Rarely weighing more than 10 to 12 pounds, Havanese are extremely companionable animals, friendly with other pets and always in a good mood. They aren't as prone to barking as other dogs their size, so they frighten small children less and are perfect for small homes and apartments.

10 Gordon setter If you're looking for a dog that will respond immediately to commands and learn good behaviors, a Gordon setter is right up your alley. These dogs are obedient to a fault, never aggressive, and will make friends with other dogs and even cats. They do need lots of exercise and firm boundaries, so start the training process right away.

10 Healthiest Breeds

While the healthiest dogs often are mutts, these purebreds also are less likely to need trips to the veterinarian. Of course, simply choosing a breed less likely to have health problems is not enough. Be sure to check with your breeder to find out what health screens and DNA tests should be conducted to minimize the chance that a health problem will affect your dog.

1 **Basenji** Basenjis are known for their inability to bark, but they also enjoy long lives with few health problems. The most common problems for this breed are hypothyroidism and hip dysplasia, both of which can be treated, depending on the severity of the problem.

2 **Shiba Inu** These small, hardy dogs have few health problems, but the problems they do have can be difficult to resolve. Patellar luxation, a condition that allows the kneecap to easily pop out of place, can cause pain and difficulty for Shibas. Screening Shibas for this condition and removing those affected from the gene pool are the best defenses against problems within the breed.

3 **Chihuahua** These small dogs can have a lifespan that is double that of extra-large dog breeds. Hypothyroidism and patellar luxation are both common Chihuahua health problems, but these remain relatively uncommon when the dogs are purchased from reputable breeders.

4 **Bichon frise** The bichon frise is a generally healthy breed, and those health conditions that are prevalent within these dogs are not life-threatening. However, bichons do get allergies and bladder stones, two conditions that require regular, ongoing treatment.

5 **Australian cattle dog** An Australian cattle dog holds the record for longest lifespan, at an astounding 29 years. These dogs exhibit few health problems, but you should be on the lookout for progressive retinal atrophy, a problem that can cause blindness.

6 **Poodle** Poodles are a hardy dog breed with very few health problems. Hip dysplasia is a concern, but prebreeding health screenings can greatly reduce the chances of this problem. Standard poodles may be subject to bloat, a potentially fatal problem that occurs when the stomach flips inside the dog.

7 **Beagle** As dog breeds go, beagles are energetic and healthy. However, they are not immune to problems such as seizure disorders and allergies.

8 **Border collie** Border collies were bred to be hardy working dogs, and most require very little veterinary care. Hip dysplasia and collie eye anomaly are the most common health problems.

9 **Greyhound** Greyhounds can easily develop dental problems, but regular brushing, cleaning and a high-quality food can help you avoid any major problems. Luckily, other health problems with this dog are fairly rare.

10 **Doberman pinscher** These intelligent dogs once were overbred due to excessive popularity, but now with new tests, many health problems have been eliminated. This breed can inherit both cardiomyopathy and Wobbler's syndrome, two life-threatening illnesses that do not have screening processes.

Top 5 Breeds for Senior Citizens

Research shows that senior citizens can benefit from pets a great deal, both mentally and physically. Besides providing companionship, pets reduce depression and stress, lower blood pressure, encourage activity and increase the opportunity for social interaction. If you're a dog person but you've been thinking pet ownership might be too much work, here are five dog breeds you will definitely want to look at.

1 **Pug** This is an ideal dog for senior citizens because of the wonderful company pugs provide. Since pugs are one of the smaller dog breeds, they can live comfortably in small senior housing. Pugs have a sweet temperament and are very affectionate. They'll play with you as much as you want and then settle down to cuddle when you're tired. Pugs are generally well behaved, so you won't have to worry about coming home to a messy apartment. But pugs are not for everyone, as they shed a lot compared to other breeds. If you don't like vacuuming, a pug may not be the right dog for you.

2 **Miniature schnauzer** This is another small, perky dog that makes a good companion for seniors. They're also good with children; if you have grandchildren who visit a lot, this is an excellent choice among dog breeds. Miniature schnauzers are energetic, affectionate and relatively easy to train. They can, however, be overly aggressive with other dogs. This may not be a good choice if you live in an area that is home to a lot of larger dogs.

3 **Yorkshire terrier** Here is an extremely adaptable, toy-size dog breed. Yorkies are vivacious, intelligent, loyal and affectionate. However, they do require a good amount of grooming; if you want low maintenance, look elsewhere. Yorkies also jump and yip a lot, which can frighten little ones. If you have small grandchildren who visit often, another breed might be a better choice.

4 **Cocker spaniel** This is a relatively small dog for a sporting dog, but it's bigger than the other breeds on this list and requires more exercise. For this reason, it's not an ideal apartment dog. If you own your own home, however, the cocker spaniel could be a great match. It's especially well suited for seniors who live alone because it makes an excellent watchdog.

5 **Chihuahua** This is one of the tiniest dog breeds in the world, making it an obvious consideration for seniors without a lot of room. Chihuahuas love attention and petting. If you're looking for a dog to shower with affection, consider this breed. Chihuahuas are fiercely loyal to their owners and excel at combating loneliness. However, they can be aggressive and jumpy, and as a result should only be allowed to play with small grandchildren if they have been properly trained.

10 Most Unusual Designer Breeds

While some designer dogs, such as the puggle, have become household names, others are just beginning to attract attention. For now, designer dogs have been deemed hybrids: offspring of two purebred dogs. Because designer dogs lack necessary breed refinements, the American Kennel Club has not yet recognized any as official dog breeds.

While designer dogs inherit breed traits from their parents, breeders cannot predict which of those characteristics each dog will adopt. That's why it's important to research the personality and appearance of both parental breeds to get an idea of what to expect. However, even dogs within the same litter may vary widely.

For pet owners willing to risk unpredictable personalities and appearances, some of these designer dogs may be appealing.

1 **Poovanese** This designer dog combines two popular city breeds—the Havanese and poodle—to create a small, lightweight dog.

2 **Cava-Tzu** Breeders combine the Cavalier King Charles spaniel and the shih tzu, purebred companion dogs, to create this hybrid.

3 **Saint Dane** The Saint Dane combines two of the largest recognized dog breeds: the Great Dane and the Saint Bernard.

4 **Schweenie** The Schweenie combines the bloodlines of the dachshund and shih tzu. This dog gets part of its name from the dachshund's nickname: the wiener dog.

5 **Rottle** The intelligent poodle is bred with the physically vigorous rottweiler to create a rottle.

6 **Shar-Poo** A miniature poodle is bred with a shar-pei to create this unique dog.

7 **Sharp Eagle** While you may expect an animal called a sharp eagle to have feathers at the very least, it's merely a hybrid of a beagle and Chinese shar-pei.

8 **English King** While not a member of British royalty, this dog is produced by breeding two English dog breeds: the Cavalier King Charles and an English toy spaniel.

9 **Dorkie** The dorkie combines two popular small breeds: the dachshund and the Yorkshire terrier.

10 **Beabull** Breeding two dogs with disparate personalities, the tranquil bulldog and the excitable beagle, creates this designer dog.

10 Best Breeds for Allergy Sufferers

Allergies don't have to get in the way of your enjoyment of pet ownership, especially if you're a dog person. The following is a list of dog breeds that are known to be best for allergy sufferers.

1 **American hairless terrier** As you'd guess from the name, this dog was bred intentionally to be hypoallergenic. It has no hair or dander, so it is the best breed out there for allergy sufferers. People who have reactions to other breeds that are supposed to be good for allergies usually do fine with the American hairless terrier.

2 **Bichon frise** This is one of the more widely available dog breeds for allergy sufferers. The bichon frise's double coat minimizes the amount of dander it sheds, which, in turn, reduces the potential for allergic reactions to this dog.

3 **Chinese crested hairless** This is a popular show dog, but the hairless version of this breed is also popular among allergy sufferers. It does have some hair on its head, feet and tail. However, the majority of its body is hairless, thus reducing shedding.

4 **Giant schnauzer** If you or someone in your family is an allergy sufferer but you'd prefer a large dog, look no further than the giant schnauzer. Like the bichon, this dog has two coats, meaning it sheds less dander than other breeds.

5 **Irish water spaniel** This is another large breed with two coats. The Irish water spaniel is a great family pet, and also is the best choice if you're looking for a hypoallergenic hunting dog.

6 **Maltese** The Maltese would not strike you as being a good dog for allergies just from looking at it, as long silky hair is its most prominent feature. However, it sheds very little, making it one of the best dog breeds for allergy sufferers. The long silky hair does require grooming, though, so take that into consideration.

7 **Miniature poodle** Most of the new "designer hybrid" dogs have poodle somewhere in their ancestry. For most of them, that is because the poodle makes for a dog that's easy on allergies. Why not skip the experiments and go straight to the source? Poodles of any kind shed very little, but choose the miniature version to minimize shedding even more.

8 **Portuguese water dog** This is a working dog bred to assist fishermen on the Iberian peninsula. If you need a workhorse breed that doesn't exacerbate allergies, this is the one for you because it sheds even less than poodles.

9 **Shih tzu** It may have a hard name to spell, but it's easy on allergy sufferers. The shih tzu sheds very little, but it does have long hair that needs to be groomed frequently, so keep that in mind if you're considering this breed.

10 **Yorkshire terrier** This is one of the most popular breeds in America today, and that's largely due to its hypoallergenic qualities. A Yorkie makes an excellent pet for families with older children (their jumping and yapping may scare smaller children). They're also ideal for people who live alone as they become very attached to their owners. Yorkies shed very little hair, but they do require regular grooming.

10 Best Breeds for City Dwellers

Just because you live in an apartment doesn't mean you have to be a cat person or get a pocket-size pooch. As long as dogs receive adequate daily exercise, many adapt well to city living.

1 **Labrador retriever** The most popular dog in America, the Labrador retriever ranks number one for city dwellers. This breed requires daily exercise, and fortunately, it is extremely tolerant of people and new experiences, which are essential traits for a city dog.

2 **Poodle** The poodle—available in standard, miniature and toy sizes—offers options to city dwellers who may not have the space for a large dog. All poodles are fiercely intelligent and easily trained by even amateur dog owners.

3 **Dachshund** The dachshund's small size makes it ideal for many city dwellers. Unlike other dog breeds, a dachshund does not require daily walks. However, apartment dwellers should know that dachshunds can be extremely vocal and prone to barking, making training a necessity.

4 **French bulldog** French bulldogs were bred specifically to be lapdogs, making them ideal for owners who like to take their pets everywhere. The French bulldog is a playful breed, but it does not require much exercise.

5 **Yorkshire terrier** The Yorkshire terrier is a small breed with a hypoallergenic coat. While the Yorkie is easy to carry throughout the city, its fragility makes it unsuitable for young children.

6 **Cavalier King Charles spaniel** Featured on *Sex and the City* as Charlotte York's dog, the Cavalier King Charles spaniel was bred as a luxury dog in England. This dog breed's small stature and gentle personality make it a winner for city dwellers who would like to show off their dog.

7 **Golden retriever** Daily walks are a requirement for city dwellers who own this hunting breed, but many who own this dog find its outgoing personality makes walking a pleasurable experience. Care should be taken to socialize young dogs, but even adult dogs can quickly adapt to city living with proper training.

8 **Havanese** Recognized as the national dog of Cuba, the Havanese is a friendly, small dog with an affectionate nature. Although considered a toy breed, the Havanese requires regular exercise beyond daily play.

9 **Shih tzu** Small and spunky, the shih tzu easily adapts to small places. Unlike many other dog breeds, the shih tzu requires little exercise, but good obedience training is essential to avoid behavioral problems. Dog owners also should budget for monthly grooming appointments.

10 **Bulldog** While bulldogs initially were bred for bull baiting, the modern breed is exceedingly gentle, and these dogs make good companions for children. They can reach 50 pounds, making them a fairly large breed. Bulldogs require little exercise.

Choosing a Dog for Your Dog

Getting Fido a playmate may be a good idea, but choosing the right companion for any dog can be a difficult process. Just like with human relationships, there are no guarantees that two dogs will hit it off. Still, with some careful planning, you have a great chance of bringing home a dog your dog will love.

Do your research

Think about the overall activity level and personality of your dog when looking for a companion. Some dogs like roughhousing; others prefer to sleep. Don't think that picking an energetic dog will encourage your existing couch potato to get some exercise. It's more likely that your existing dog will become annoyed and ignore the intruder. If you have a purebred dog, consider the same breed of dog, or a breed that has similar characteristics. For a mixed-breed dog, honestly assessing your current dog's personality becomes even more important in finding the correct match.

Think about an adult dog

While many pet owners may think choosing a puppy is a safe choice, many adult dogs don't have the patience to help raise a young dog. Instead, think about picking an adult dog that has good manners and is well socialized. Many dog rescues will allow you to foster a dog, making it a great option if you are looking for a companion dog. Don't be afraid to try several dogs to get the right match for your household; all rescues want the best possible fit for their dogs. When choosing a dog, look for a canine that will be submissive to the other dogs in your house. This will ensure that the existing dogs will help you enforce any house rules that are set in place. A new, dominant dog can cause bad behavior by influencing your existing canines.

It's a companion, not a substitute

Don't make the mistake of thinking that choosing a dog for your existing dog will excuse a lack of human leadership. Dogs are likely to pick up bad habits from one another, making it even more important that you enforce the house rules and practice basic training commands with each dog. You should also enforce the pack structure within your home. The dominant dog should be fed and greeted first. Although this may seem unfair to the submissive dog, dogs do not perceive this as favoritism. Dogs prefer cues that reinforce their position in the pack, even if they are not the alpha dogs. This helps them feel secure and prevents infighting within the group.

Consult a behaviorist

After choosing a dog, get a dog behaviorist to look at both of the dogs interacting before making a final decision. An experienced behaviorist will be able to anticipate any possible problems before a fight or other trouble occurs. She may also make training recommendations to help ease the transition into a two-dog household.

5 Online Pet Name Finders

Looking for the perfect name for your pet? There are thousands of possibilities. Fortunately, the World Wide Web might have the answer. The following are five pet name websites that can help you tap your inner creative genius.

1 Bowwow.com.au This site is a bit colorful and sometimes difficult to navigate, but it offers something that other sites don't: name meanings. In addition to searching its extensive database for the perfect name, you can also find out what each name means to help you find something suitable. You can click on the search field in the left navigation bar to search for pet names, male and female. You can even choose categories such as religious, foreign, sport names and nicknames. Once you have a list of possibilities, you can search each one to find out exactly what it means. It will even tell you if any Beanie Babies share that name, or if there are any pop culture references.

2 Funpetnames.com If you are looking for a better organized website, this is probably right up your alley. Funpetnames.com is focused more on category: male or female, geographical region, famous names, type of animal and a host of other ways to search.
Many of the names found here are also popular choices for people, too. Although this site lists the meanings of the pet name you choose, the descriptions are more limited and are related mostly to foreign translations. For example, the name "Ammitai" means "truth" in Hebrew. It also has lists of popular monikers throughout the ages.

3 Petnamesworld.com A little zany and a lot of fun, this site is a great resource for parents to peruse with their kids. Adorable little icons for each type of pet combined with wacky fonts and colorful backgrounds make this an enjoyable website to search. It is also informative, with more than 11,000 names in its database. The search engine is more limited, however, and you can only find names according to male or female animals, and alphabetically. You can keep a record of your favorite names for future reference, and it also has an extensive list of links to other informative pet-related websites.

4 Mypetnames.com Although pet names are certainly a focus for this website, there is a host of other information about breeds, wild animals and other cool facts. It won't win any design awards with its plain black, gray and white colors, but it is a bit easier to navigate than other sites and offers a good deal of information. This is the place to go if you're looking for a name for an exotic pet such as a parrot or reptile. You'll have fun browsing through all the ideas, which are ranked according to popularity.

5 Pet-net.net If you are looking for names related to a particular country or ethnicity, this is the website you will want to use. Browse for Celtic, French, German, American, Japanese and even Native American names in its extensive database. It also has a bookstore if you need a larger collection of possibilities.

Things to Consider When Choosing a Name

If you have recently adopted a dog, one of the first things you will need to figure out is what to call her. While this may seem very easy, keep in mind that your dog will carry the name you choose for her entire life. Here are some of the things to consider when choosing a dog name.

- **Keep the name the dog came with.** If you adopted the dog, chances are she already has a name. Keeping this name can make the transition to your new home much easier for the dog—if some stranger is constantly addressing her by a new name, a confusing situation can become even more so. If you absolutely hate the name the dog has, consider the following.

- **Select a name you're comfortable saying.** One factor to keep in mind when choosing a dog name is how easy it is to say. Consider names with two syllables or less; these names will prove easy to use repeatedly, whether during training sessions or when calling her name to get her attention. Of course, if you prefer a longer name, you always can train your dog to respond to a shortened nickname (i.e., Nick vs. Nicholas). In fact, nicknames are a great way to convey your feelings toward your dog, particularly when used in response to either good or bad behavior. Just remember to be reasonable in selecting a name for your new pet, and avoid any name that you will be embarrassed to say aloud in public.

- **Know the effects of certain sounds and words.** Dogs are attuned to hearing at higher frequencies than humans, according to psychologist and author Stanley Coren. Whereas humans can hear sounds at a maximum frequency of 20 kHz, dogs hear sounds up to 45 kHz. "S" sounds are much more compelling to dogs. Names such as Alice and Samson, for instance, may be good monikers for this reason. Experts also advise against using names that sound similar to obedience terms, such as "no," which can lead to confusion and negative associations.

- **Look into the history of the breed.** If you have a Portuguese water dog, which is the type of dog the Obamas adopted, consider a nautical theme. If you have a Scottish terrier, consider a Scottish name. This can open up some possibilities, and give your dog a name that is distinctive from the rest of the crowd. It's important that 10 dogs don't come running when you call your dog.

Whether you hear a name in a song or think a certain word really describes your dog, it's important to put these and other tips to good use before selecting a name. Adopting a pet is a huge commitment, and you owe it to yourself and your furry friend to choose a dog name that suits you both.

5 Tips for Choosing a Pet Name

Choosing a unique and fitting pet name can be challenging, especially if you've just adopted a pet from the shelter or another family and it already has a name. If you're naming a recently born animal, you will need to figure out what distinct personality traits or characteristics the pet has so that her name reflects her nature.

1 **Consider a famous name.** Famous pets in history may be a good source of inspiration for naming your pet. If you want to turn your pet into a little celebrity, consider naming her after a famous pet, or even a famous character in history. Old Yeller, Lassie, Buddy, Benji, Rover and Rufus are just a few notable names.

2 **Pick out a certain characteristic or personality trait.** Most pet owners choose a pet name based on their pet's personality. For example, a dog that is especially affectionate, or one that runs very fast, may earn a name such as "Sweetie" or "Speedy." You can have fun with your pet's name if he has a dominating trait.

3 **Choose a name that begins with a hard consonant.** Names that begin with a *K, T, M* or *S* are easier to recognize than those that start with a vowel or other letters. Dogs in particular will pick up these names easily in a crowd or other noisy setting. You will also want to make sure the name doesn't rhyme with or sound like a word you might use in training.

4 **Name your pet after a famous fictional character.** If you like the sound of a fictional character's name, practice calling it a few times to see if it might be a good match for your pet. Many pet owners choose a name from children's books, cartoons, TV programs or their favorite movie.

5 **Keep it short and sweet.** Very long names can make it hard to train your pet. Most dogs are very sensitive to noise, and only need to hear the first few syllables of their name to react. If you do choose an especially long name, consider shortening it or using a nickname so that it only ends up being one or two syllables.

It can take some time to find the perfect name for your pet, but you will need to find one that fits your pet's personality, and one that doesn't make you cringe each time you say it. Practice saying a few different names out loud and see if your pet seems to respond to any of them naturally. If she perks up and pays attention after a particular name, you've found the right match.

Unusual Dog Names

- **Rush Limbark** After watching the power that a certain conservative radio host had over her dogs, one pet owner named her next pooch after Rush Limbaugh. Rescued after Hurricane Katrina, this dog also enjoys sitting down and listening to the human Rush bark at liberals over the air.

- **Sophie Touch & Pee** One woman's golden retriever gets so excited at times that the pet can't control her bladder. An unfortunate veterinarian found this out during one visit with the dog.

- **Peanut Wigglebutt** A woman adopted the runt of a litter of dachshunds. She thought the dog looked like a little peanut. Her new pet gets so excited about attention that she wags her tail hard enough to lose her balance.

- **Low Jack** A LoJack is an innovative vehicle recovery system used by police, but "Low Jack" is the name of one pet owner's bulldog/corgi mix. The owner gave him the affectionate name because his short legs make him walk low to the ground.

- **Sirius Lee Handsome** No information on this name's origin was available, but since Sirius also is known as the "dog star," the owner must be an astronomy buff who thinks his or her canine friend is pretty good-looking.

10 Popular Male Pet Names

10 Brandon Little Punky Brewster had a golden retriever named Brandon during the run of her titular series. This television pooch was named in honor of Brandon Tartikoff, the head of programming for NBC at the time.

9 Tramp His name may have been Tramp, but this furry, fuzzy canine was the beloved pet of the Douglas family on *My Three Sons.* Tramp is one of the more unusual pet names, but it seemed to fit this affectionate mixed breed.

8 Duke Jed Clampett loved his bloodhound, even though Duke couldn't really rouse himself to go chasing after rabbits. Duke was a mainstay of *The Beverly Hillbillies* for most of the show's run.

7 Petey This pit bull is still famous, decades after his debut in the *Little Rascals/Our Gang* comedy shorts. His real name was Pal, but he became famous as Petey, the faithful pup with a black circle around his eye.

6 Snoopy The creation of the late, great cartoonist Charles Schulz, Snoopy is one dog with a rich fantasy life, imagining himself to be a great writer and a World War I fighter pilot. This may be one of the most popular pet names around.

5 Buddy British slang for "messenger," it would be great if you could train a dog named Buddy to retrieve the mail and newspaper on a regular basis. In American slang, it also is an affectionate term for a close friend.

4 Marmaduke This cartoon Great Dane may look imposing, but he's all heart...and tongue. Marmaduke's size makes him a bit clumsy, and he has trouble controlling himself when the neighbors are having a barbecue.

3 Benji On the *Petticoat Junction* TV series in the 1960s, the three Bradley sisters had a dog that was simply called "Dog" for the duration of the show. Known as Higgins in real life, this canine achieved even greater fame as the original star of the *Benji* films.

2 Eddie Arguably the most famous Jack Russell terrier on television, little Eddie tormented high-strung radio psychologist Frasier Crane for the better part of a decade on *Frasier.*

1 Marley Author John Grogan wrote a bestselling book about Marley, his family's lovable, frustrating canine companion. Grogan's book also inspired a popular holiday movie starring Owen Wilson and Jennifer Aniston.

10 Popular Female Pet Names

10 Zoe In Greek, the name Zoe means "life," which is what many pets bring into the home.

9 Sophie Another name with Greek origins, Sophie means "wisdom," which is hard to believe when your best friend is chewing on the sofa. This wise name is quite popular in the United Kingdom and Austria.

8 Bailey A name that can be given to males or females, the name Bailey has roots in jolly ol' England and typically refers to a steward or public official. It also means the outer wall of a castle or the area between two outer castle walls.

7 Chloe Here is another word with Greek roots. It means "blooming," which could be a fitting name for an ever-growing furry friend. Another interpretation is "young shoot," such as grass or the buds on a tree.

6 Ginger England is back on the board with Ginger, a name that is short for Virginia. It can mean "pure and virginal" or simply point out that your pet has reddish fur. Virginia is derived from the Latin word for "spring-like" or "flourishing."

5 Sadie In both English and Hebrew, Sadie can be short for Sarah, which means "princess." Over the last eight years, Sadie has shown a slow increase in popularity, ending up at No. 109 on the Social Security Administration's list of popular girls' names for 2008.

4 Lucy With roots in Italy, Lucy is short for Lucia, a beautiful name that means "graceful light" or "illumination." In Russia, it is an affectionate nickname for Tatyana.

3 Daisy In Old English, Daisy means "day's eye," and also is the name of a popular flower. Among pet names, Daisy is great for a bright, spunky dog. Because *marguerite* is the French word for daisy, Margaret has become one of the more formal versions of this flowery name.

2 Maggie A Scottish name, Maggie is short for Margaret, the "pearl" of the family. In America, Maggie has been hovering around the No. 200 position on the list of popular girls' names for the last several years.

1 Molly This is another English name that originates from the Gaelic Maili ("bitter"). Some parents use it as an affectionate form of the name Mary.

TRAINING YOUR DOG

Now that you've found a canine friend, it's crucial to take the steps to ensure that you'll live together harmoniously. A word to the wise: Start early. Whether the dog is 2 months old or 2 years old when you acquire him is not as important as whether you begin the training process swiftly and continue it consistently. Training need not be seen as a difficult process, but rather as a way to get to know each other —and to show who's boss. Dogs are pack animals; they're hardwired to expect a particular place in the group. Now that your family is his pack, it's essential that you set clear boundaries from the outset to establish his place in the household so that everyone will be content.

10 Most Intelligent Breeds

Choosing an intelligent dog breed is important for a variety of reasons. Among other considerations, a dog's level of intelligence helps indicate how easy it will be to live with and how much attention it will require from you. Here are 10 of the most intelligent dog breeds.

1 **Shetland sheepdog** This breed is accepted widely as one of the smartest. It was bred to wrangle sheep and cattle, a job that requires a high level of brain function. More than anything else, these dogs enjoy attention from people.

2 **Doberman pinscher** Dobermans are loyal dogs known for being easy to train and for their great skill range. While Doberman pinschers' temperaments can vary greatly, they are loyal dogs that work well in a family setting, despite their intimidating appearance.

3 **Golden retriever** A golden retriever's intellect often is reflected in its ability to obey its master. Golden retrievers use this wonderful affinity for obedience to excel at performing tricks.

4 **Border collie** While this breed is very intelligent, it requires an active pet owner and lifestyle. Border collies require large yards and lots of activity, and they are masterful at showcasing their skills in dog shows and on farms.

5 **Poodle** The poodle loves to be around people. These dogs are known for being easy to train and willing to learn new skills. These qualities make poodles excellent participants in dog shows and wonderful companions at home.

6 **Rottweiler** While these dogs' intimidating nature is well-known, rottweilers are regarded as some of the most intelligent guard dogs available. They are intensely loyal to their families and are known for their willingness to be trained.

7 **German shepherd** They may be best recognized for their athletic abilities and bravery, but German shepherds also rank high in the intelligence department. Their ability to function as protective guard dogs stems from their ability to be easily trained.

8 **Labrador retriever** When you are looking for a dog that is good-natured and intelligent, the Labrador retriever is a breed that jumps to the top of the list. They make wonderful family dogs, but Labrador retrievers do require attention from their owners, regular exercise and a controlled diet. Their inviting appearance makes them particularly popular with families.

9 **Australian cattle dog** When you want an easy-to-train dog that can handle a high level of activity, the Australian cattle dog is probably your best fit. Like the border collie, these dogs were bred to herd cattle and require a high level of activity. This makes them perfect for active families with big yards.

10 **Papillon** Many small dogs are known for their feisty natures. This is not the case with the tiny papillon, which is easy to train and well-known for its affinity for people.

Pet Training 101: Good Dog

Your puppy has broken into the pantry for a fifth time, and now he's staring at you with those *I love you* eyes, trying to pretend that nothing has happened. As always, you find yourself thinking, *I should take him to a trainer.* But you hate to fork over the $200 (or more!) fee. Don't worry. We've got everything you need to tame your savage beast.

Puppies have a natural curiosity and lust for life, so you have to channel that energy and make it work for you, says Kevin Behan, author of *Natural Dog Training.*

Step 1 Establish a solid framework for effective training. Make sure your home is a calm, safe space for your new puppy. Stroke and handle him as often as possible so he gets used to human contact.

Step 2 Start with the basics. First, teach him his name. Every time he responds to it, give him a treat. Next, get him used to the leash. Carry him to a spot away from the house, and let him lead you back. If he tugs the leash, turn your body the opposite way. He'll follow you, then bound ahead.

Step 3 Train him to sit, stay and heel by holding treats at waist height and moving them in a slow circle, mesmerizing him. When you hold food above a puppy's head, he'll automatically sit or settle back on his hips. Gradually incorporate hand gestures and verbal commands. Once he's mastered that, teach him to come by trotting backward quickly (leash in your left hand, a treat visible in your right) while repeating the word *come.* Reward him every time he obeys.

Training 101: Dos and Don'ts

Dog training can be difficult for the uninitiated—both owner and pet—but it's ultimately a rewarding experience for those who persist. These dog training dos and don'ts will help you avoid common pitfalls when training your dog.

- **Do** find a distraction-free location. Always start learning a new command at a location that is free from distractions. This will allow your dog to focus on learning. After she understands the command, introduce distractions slowly.

- **Don't** forget to reward for good behavior. Many dog owners reward their dogs while learning, but quickly forget to reward their dog for continued good behavior. Commands like "stay" and "drop it" are potentially lifesaving. It is important to reinforce the importance of following these commands every time you use them by rewarding appropriately.

- **Do** use both hand and verbal cues. Blindness and loss of hearing are common afflictions for older dogs. By using both cues, you can retain the ability to communicate with your pet.

- **Don't** plan on sessions longer than 20 minutes. Expecting a young dog to focus on learning for longer than 20 minutes is unfair. Instead, try to find 20 minutes to work with your dog each day. As your dog reaches maturity, her attention span will grow, allowing you to extend sessions if you wish.

- **Do** practice commands at different locations. Young dogs don't know that "sit" and "stay" are universal, no matter where you are. For them, "stay" practiced inside the house may have little connection to a "stay" in the backyard. Try practicing at various places so your dog will associate the command with your voice and hand signals, not the location.

- **Don't** use an excited voice to gain your pet's attention. An excited voice may help you get your dog to come to you at first, but you shouldn't be competing for your dog's attention. Use a firm, calm voice to issue commands and do not repeat the cue. This will ensure that the dog will come to you even when something else she sees is more exciting.

- **Do** reinforce pack behavior at all times. Your dog should perceive you to be head of your house before you begin training. Building that relationship requires that you reinforce good behavior and punish bad behavior consistently. Making sure your dog is heeling during regular walks is also a good way to build that bond.

- **Don't** be afraid to go to a dog trainer. Even if you don't enroll in a standard eight-week obedience course, consider scheduling a few appointments with a dog trainer. A trainer will be able to give you insight into your dog's mind that will make training easier.

- **Do** stay calm no matter what. Dog training requires a lot of patience and positive reinforcement. Never yell at or hit your dog; you want to inspire loyalty, not fear.

- **Don't** stop until progress has been made. Many owners become frustrated and stop training before the dog has learned the command. This can reinforce bad behavior in a dog, making her think that acting up can get her out of training.

- **Don't** ever say your pup's name in anger, as a reprimand. It undermines the relationship you're trying to build with him.

- 🐾 **Do** create a "relax zone" (inside) and a "play zone" (outside). Many puppy problems (chewing furniture, peeing in corners) can be averted by reinforcing these zones. Playing indoors winds dogs up. Let dogs loose outside, where you can shape their energy and enthusiasm to your ends.

- 🐾 **Don't** yell at your pooch when he makes a mistake. It can scare him and make him fearful of people.

- 🐾 **Do** teach your pup the meaning of *No*. Put food in a bowl and lower it to the floor. As your dog gets excited, say "No" calmly but firmly and pull the bowl away. Repeat a few more times. Eventually his excitement will fade and he'll lie down. Now set the bowl down. The result? Your puppy learns that *No* means *Stop, be patient.*

Training FAQs

Teaching your dog to sit may seem like a simple task, but learning even simple commands represents an enormous challenge for most dogs. By understanding some basic facts about your dog's mental processes, you can work to overcome obstacles together.

Why is it so hard for my dog to learn?

Most obedience training goes against the instincts of your dog. Commands such as "drop it" are difficult to teach dogs because it goes against their essential nature. They want to keep whatever they have because there is a strong instinct that if they drop it, another dog will take it. For tricks that are difficult for your dog to grasp, try talking to a dog behaviorist. These professionals will be able to explain why your dog is reluctant to follow your instructions.

What are the two most important commands for my dog to learn?

"Drop it" and "come" are pretty important. Dogs may find themselves in dangerous situations that require they immediately obey you. Saving your dog's life by preventing

her from swallowing something dangerous or running into traffic is the most important result of good obedience training. For this reason, practicing with your dog every day, even into adulthood, is essential.

How old does my dog have to be before she obeys me?

Many owners expect too much from their young dogs. Basic command obedience within 15 feet is great for dogs under a year. Many owners think that an eight-week obedience class will teach their dog all she needs to know for life. However, young dogs don't have the attention span to fully master some commands such as "come" with distractions; they have to be at least a year old. Consider the basic training class as a foundation for learning for your dog.

Is my dog just a slow learner?

Group training classes may have you wondering why your dog is the last to catch on, but there may be good reasons for your dog to be slow. Dog training is a snap for breeds such as poodles and border collies, which are both highly intelligent and eager to please. For other dogs, understanding and consistent obedience come more slowly.

When will my dog be fully trained?

Dog training should never end. Try 15 minutes with your dog every day to reinforce commands. Otherwise your dog may forget commands over time. The key to these dog training lessons is to keep it light; use treats generously and slow down to reteach your dog if she becomes confused. Dogs will often look forward to these sessions as a time to bond with you.

Training 101: Using Positive Reinforcement

Puppies and older dogs like to play, and without proper guidance, they will take ownership of your favorite pair of slippers, the pantry, your garden hose and anything else that isn't nailed down. One of the easiest and most effective ways to stop bad behavior and encourage good actions is through positive reinforcement. You'll build a foundation of trust and respect with your dog while saving your furniture from his relentless jaws.

1 **Use food.** The most common type of positive reinforcement used in dog training is food. It's the same concept as rewarding yourself with a Starbucks Frappuccino after a particularly grueling workout or an ice cream cone when you've completed a project at work. However, there are other forms of positive reinforcement that can work equally well. If you don't like the idea of popping out a dog biscuit after every incident of good behavior, you can use petting, verbal praise or a round of fetch as positive reinforcement.

   The point is to reward good behavior with something your dog enjoys. The benefit of food is that most dogs are motivated by a tasty treat and will automatically look to you for more. This keeps their attention focused on you and allows for constant training throughout the day.

2 **Give yourself time to learn.** Like any method of dog training, positive reinforcement takes time to master, and it is perfectly acceptable to make a few mistakes. If you've never taken a training class or read any literature, expect a learning curve and don't beat yourself up for making mistakes.

3 **Teach key words.** You'll want your dog to understand and respond to certain commands, and the earlier you expose him to those commands, the better. According to The Humane Society of the United States, some of the most common words used in dog training are *sit, stay, heel, come, down, off* and *leave it.*

4 **Lead by example.** Show your dog what each word means by helping him respond correctly. For example, if he is on the couch and you don't want him to have furniture privileges, say "off." Then, gently guide your dog back to the floor. Once he is there, praise him, or give him a treat immediately to show that was what you wanted.

5 **Be consistent.** Respond to each behavior the same way every time your dog does it. Training your dog is not effective unless you are consistent as often as possible, which means your pooch can't be welcome on the couch only sometimes.

6 **Never stop teaching.** A bored dog can be a destructive dog. Once you've established the correct responses to the commands you want your dog to learn, keep the lessons coming. For example, you may want to praise Fido every time he settles down with a chew toy because he is using an approved item rather than the armoire you inherited from Grandma. This is especially important with smart and/or high-energy dogs, such as border collies. If you don't keep them interested, they'll find something to do—and you might not like the result.

Pet Care 101: Disciplining a New Dog

An important topic in pet care is how to introduce a dog to his new life in your household. Bringing a new dog into your home will hopefully enrich your life and his. Given enough attention and care, your new dog will happily become part of the family. However, teaching your dog the rules and routines of your home is an important part of the transition process. Disciplining your new dog does not mean punishing him, but rather teaching him what behavior you expect from him. Proper pet care is not complete without teaching your dog a few manners.

- **Lay out the ground rules.** What basic manners do you expect your dog to have? Consistency is an important part of training your dog, so all family members should be on the same page about how your dog should behave. For example, will your new dog be allowed on the furniture? Will he be allowed to beg at the dinner table, or will he be expected to remain outside of the room entirely? If you decide that your dog won't be allowed on the couch but your kids encourage him to join them there while they watch TV, then your new pet will be confused. Consistency is important in any training.

- **"Yes" is more important than "no."** Positive reinforcement is the quickest way to train your dog. For example, praise him when he goes to the bathroom outside rather than inside. It can be easier to change behaviors by praising the behavior you want to encourage rather than punishing the unwanted action. For example, if you don't like that he plays tug-of-war with toys, teach him to fetch toys instead. You can do this by throwing the toy and praising him when he brings it back to you.

- **Learn to say "no" effectively.** Sometimes you will have to teach your new dog which behaviors are not appropriate. Your pet will probably make many mistakes when he first moves in. When telling your dog he is doing something wrong, you should not use his name to get his attention. Your dog should associate his name with positive reinforcement only. To a dog, his name is what you use to tell him to "come" or to tell him that he's a good dog. Imagine how confusing it would be to be told to "come" and then have "no" shouted at you as you start to respond. So, you will have to get your dog's attention by standing where he can see you or touching him gently on his neck with your fingers. Say the word "no" firmly, but do not scream it at him. You want to be calm and in control, rather than frantic or overly angry.

- **Exercise is key.** Apart from teaching your dog to behave well, appropriate pet care will go a long way toward preventing bad behavior. Dogs that are given a lot of attention and exercise are less likely to develop nervous habits such as chewing, or find annoying ways to occupy themselves such as barking for hours on end. Even small dogs need to be exercised. Simply letting your dog out in the yard does not count. Walks will help your dog work off energy, and will keep you in shape, too.

40

Training Basics: Teaching Your Dog to Stay

1 **Start with your dog on a leash.** This signals to her that you will be working together.

2 **Ask your dog to sit.** (Only teach "stay" after she understands "sit.") It is easiest for your dog to learn this command while sitting.

3 **Stand in front of your dog** with the leash in your hand.

4 **Put your hand out** in front of your dog and say "stay."

5 **Take three steps backward** so that you are about 3 feet away from your dog.

6 **Wait a moment.** If your dog does not move, continue. If she does move, say "no" and encourage her to sit in the exact same spot and try again.

7 **After your dog has stayed for five seconds without moving,** walk toward her and release her. Do this by saying "OK" and gently leading your dog a few steps away from the spot where she was sitting. Give a treat once the dog has moved.

8 **Practice this sequence** until your dog has successfully completed a stay at least three times in a row. If it has taken you 10 minutes or longer to get to this point, praise your dog and plan on working on the command again during your next dog training session. For dogs that caught on more quickly, work on the "stay" command for 10 minutes using verbal and hand cues, rewarding her each time.

9 **The goal in the next sessions** is to increase the length and distance of the stay. Start by increasing the distance to the full length of the leash, which should be about 5 feet. Once your dog has mastered the additional length, add additional time.

10 **When your dog has mastered "stay" on a leash** for at least 10 seconds, start learning "stay" off the leash. Detach the leash and start small; stand only 3 feet away. Increase the distance each session. A good goal for a dog under 1 year old is to stay for 30 seconds, 15 feet away.

11 **For older dogs,** try areas with more distractions as well as longer times and distances. Front yards, and later dog parks, are good places to start. A helper can also try to distract your dog from the "stay" command by doing something in the sight line of your dog. Never have your helper call the dog in order to distract her during dog training; this can confuse her.

5 Tips for Teaching Your Pet Her Name

After you've selected the perfect pet name, it's time to train your pet to respond to it. Teaching your pet her name can take time, especially if she had another name before becoming a part of your family. If you have a recently born pet without a name, she will need to learn that she should respond to her name when it's called.

1 **Say the name with a positive tone.** Your pet needs to associate her name with a positive experience, so you will need to say her name loudly and clearly with a very positive tone. Practice saying the name in an uplifting, loving way, so that your dog recognizes it as a positive statement. A high-pitched tone is the best way to point out that the word you are saying is very important.

2 **Don't use other words or phrases with the name.** Your pet needs to recognize her name easily, so don't talk in complete sentences using the name until she has adjusted to it. You want to say the new pet name as if your dog already knows her name. Use it to get her attention, and as a single-word command so your pet can hear it properly. Remember: Repetition is key!

3 **Set up a reward system.** Give your pet a reward each time she looks at you after you call her name so that she understands that this word has significance. Every time you say the name and your pet looks up at you or responds in any way, reward her with a treat or a pat. It won't take long for her to realize that she needs to respond to the word.

4 **Slowly increase distractions.** When your pet starts to respond to the name on a regular basis, start using the name within a sentence, or in an unfamiliar place with lots of distractions. You want to make it harder for your pet to recognize her name with more distractions so that she can respond in a real-world setting in future. Continue to praise and reward her every time she responds to her name when it's used in a sentence, or in a place with a lot of distractions.

5 **Don't use her name in a negative situation.** Avoid reprimanding your pet with her new name when she's still learning to respond to it. If you need to reprimand her, simply say "no" in a direct way. Don't link her name with the bad behavior, or she may not respond to her new name in the future.

Training 101: Housebreaking a Puppy

Housebreaking a puppy is an important part of dog training. It is easier for a housebroken dog to integrate itself into society. So how do you do it? These five dog training steps will help you housebreak your puppy. Use them consistently, and your new dog will eventually learn to relieve itself only in designated areas.

- **Designate a potty area.** Where do you want your puppy to relieve himself? Designate a potty area, and familiarize your puppy with it. This area should be the only place in or outside of your house that smells of urine or defecation. These odors will attract your puppy when he has the urge to go.

- **Set out several meals a day.** While you are housebreaking your puppy, don't leave food or water out for him to consume throughout the day. Instead, select several times a day to feed and hydrate him. Fill his food and water bowl at this time and watch him eat. This way, you can predict when he'll want to relieve himself.

- **Regulate all potty breaks.** A puppy will get the urge to urinate or defecate 10 to 20 minutes after he eats and drinks. To housebreak him, then, you must be present at every meal. Ten minutes after he eats, take him to the designated potty area. If he doesn't go in five minutes, take him back inside or away from the potty area. When you see him circling or about to squat, take him back to the designated potty area again so he can go.

- **Use praise and keywords.** When your puppy relieves himself in the designated potty area, praise him. Use the same keywords or phrase every time to attribute meaning to them. For example, say "good dog" or "good potty break." Then, be sure to express yourself with positive facial expressions and gestures. By doing this, you will motivate your puppy to continue his new behavior because he sees it pleases you.

- **Give your puppy time to learn.** Dog training articles are written often on the subject of housebreaking. The time given for housebreaking a puppy ranges from three days to six months. As a responsible dog owner, you should lean toward the longer period of time, because a puppy has to build up his ability to hold urine and defecation. As a result, he will be less apt to have an accident as he matures. If he isn't completely housebroken after six months, take him to a veterinarian for a physical exam.

Training 101: The Ins and Outs of Crate Training

Housebreaking a dog using a crate can be perceived as cruel. However, if done properly, crate training provides security and comfort to your dog. Follow these dog training steps to get your pet ready for a crate.

- **Learn why crates work.** Before you buy a crate, it is best to understand how it will help to housebreak your dog. Dogs are born with a strong desire to sleep in a den. A crate is a great man-made substitute for a den—and dogs won't want to soil where they sleep. Crates let you use this natural instinct to your advantage, helping you teach your puppy how to hold it between potty trips outside.

- **Take your puppy out for 10 to 15 minutes on a leash when on bathroom breaks.** A leash is important, because it reinforces to the dog that it is outside for a reason—to go potty. If the dog doesn't go in that time, bring her back inside, and put the puppy back in the crate for five minutes with the leash still on before taking her outside again. This tells the dog that something is amiss, and hopefully will send the message that time outside is for potty breaks. Continue the pattern until the dog goes to the bathroom. *WebVet.com* says to expect a puppy to need bathroom breaks every two to three hours during the day, and at least once or twice overnight. With each passing month, your puppy may well need fewer bathroom breaks.

- **Enforce the positive attributes of the crate.** Because crate training can be a long, frustrating process for your pet, it's important to keep your dog calm and cooperative by associating the crate with something positive. Pad the crate with soft, comfortable blankets, and place it in an area of your home that will be conducive to relaxation for your pet. Instead of forcing a hesitant dog to enter her crate, lead your pooch to her new den by creating a path of treats that stops at the back of the crate. Always speak to your dog in an uplifting tone when she is in or near the crate.

- **Introduce mealtime in the crate.** Once you have acclimated your dog to her crate, begin feeding her meals while she is inside it. Gauge your dog's comfort level; if she's still a bit hesitant, keep her food dish and water closer to the crate door. If she's freely wandering within the crate, place her bowls toward the back. When your dog gets into the habit of comfortably eating inside the crate, begin shutting the crate door, increasing the length of time you keep it closed each day.

- **Fight the rescue impulse.** After your dog has accepted the crate as her dining area, begin further crate training. Do not give in to the temptation to let her out each time she pleadingly barks or whines. She should finish her meals inside the crate.

- **Prepare to leave her alone.** Before setting out for a short trip outside your house, lead your dog to her crate by enticing her with treats. Make sure she's surrounded by positive reinforcements such as treats and toys, and be sure you have not left her in the crate for longer than 20 minutes before taking off. Start out slow; pick up dinner and come back home. Gradually work your way up to when you will go to work and leave her in her crate.

Training 101: Is Obedience School Worth It?

Obedience training might be your only option, but is it worth the cost? You'll have to invest both time and money for this type of dog training to succeed, so don't jump in without carefully considering your options.

Making the commitment Like school for your kids, obedience training does not just constitute an hour or so of your time every week. Your trainer—if you've chosen a reputable professional—will assign homework every class, and you won't make any progress unless you practice what you've learned.

Before you sign up for obedience school, consider your current schedule. Will family obligations, work and other commitments leave time for you and your pooch to go over what you learned in class? If not, you might be better off seeking other options.

Of course, you can practice what you've learned in obedience training at any time. If you can carve out 20 minutes before work or 15 minutes before you go to bed, that will be sufficient. You'll also need to attend every class, so make sure other obligations won't get in the way, or you will surely miss valuable steps in the dog training process.

Coughing up the cash Obedience school is not cheap, which means you'll have to write a check before your trainer starts to fix your puppy issues. Some classes cost as little as $150 to $200 for six weeks, while others may cost as much as $1,000. The price of obedience school will depend on how often you meet, the reputation of the trainer, your geographical location and a host of other factors. In a tough economy, many families are loathe to part with hard-earned cash.

Before you decide to go this route, call around and price several obedience schools. Ask for literature so you can compare the different trainers and make an educated decision. You don't want to go with an unknown trainer with an iffy reputation, but don't empty your bank account, either.

Evaluating the alternatives Obedience school is not the only dog training option. Many dog owners opt for do-it-yourself alternatives to save money, and many succeed beyond their wildest dreams. There are tons of books, videos, websites and other media available, so never think you're alone.

You also have to remember that obedience classes are generally limited to one family member with each dog. This often leads to an uncomfortable hierarchy where the pooch will listen to one master but none of the others. DIY solutions mean every family member gets to take part.

Before you decide whether obedience training is right for your dog, attend a class or two. Many trainers allow auditing for free or a nominal fee, which will give you an opportunity to evaluate and decide if it will work for your family. If the trainer isn't willing to let you sit in on a class, you should probably wonder why he doesn't want people watching.

Top Training Tips from the Dog Whisperer

Learn these insider tips from pack leader Cesar Millan

Cesar Millan, better known as the Dog Whisperer, is known for offering tried-and-true dog-training solutions to frustrated, struggling pet owners. Among his most helpful tips are some that are sure to have even new dog owners leading the pack in no time.

1 **Just like kids, dogs need a schedule.** Like a temper tantrum–throwing toddler without structure in its life, a dog without a set schedule is bound to become irritable and act out. Dogs need set times for interaction, exercise, feeding and training.

2 **Leadership is the foundation of training.** Dog training relies on the presence of one pack leader. A dog lover who assumes the role of pack leader will have successful training sessions.

3 **Half the battle takes place in your mind.** You must have unwavering mental strength and confidence to gain the trust and respect of your dog during training sessions. Your dog can sense if you are uncertain or fear it, so you must control situations by maintaining the role of an authoritative pack leader.

4 **Discipline and punishment are not synonymous.** Invest heavily in dog training, and there will be no need for punishment. It takes time and effort to see real improvement in your dog's behavior. Don't let your frustrations distract you from your goal to properly and successfully train your pet.

5 **A dog is a dog.** Treating a dog in a humanized manner is perhaps the cardinal sin dog lovers commit. Love your dog, but do not treat him as a baby. Only dogs that understand their role within a family unit are actually trainable. Upset the role identification, and problems are sure to ensue.

6 **Dogs need boundaries.** Follow Millan's example, and set boundaries in your home. If your dog's barking at company bothers you, make this a focal point of your training. If a dog's presence in an off-limits room annoys you, focus on this aspect of the dog's behavior instead.

7 **Consistency is key.** It is easy to let a dog get away with eating off your plate "just this once," but in so doing, you are setting a dangerous precedent. How is the dog to know that tomorrow morning this is no longer acceptable behavior?

8 **Get all family members on board.** It takes a household to properly train a dog. You, your partner and all household members need to be on the same page when it comes to acceptable and unacceptable behavior. While there is only one pack leader, the other family members still are dominant to the dog, and they must treat their relationship with it as such.

9 **Start today.** It is never too early or too late to start working with a dog. Whether your canine companion is a puppy or a more mature dog, commit to start today and achieve with your dog what Millan refers to as "balance between people and dogs."

Why Does My Dog...

Make weird sounds? Scoot across the rug? Chase his own tail? Top experts explain.

You live with them, play with them and even sleep next to them, but if you're like most pet owners, you often can't figure out why your pets do what they do. Although some behaviors may seem bizarre, there is a meaning to each of them. "Pay attention," urges Cesar Millan, host of *Dog Whisperer* on the National Geographic Channel. "You can break the code." Here's why your dog...

Runs through the house like he's on fire

You're calmly watching TV when your dog bolts past like a shot out of the blue. You have no idea where he's going or what set him off. All you know is that suddenly he's gone nuts.

Don't ship him off to the psych ward just yet. The poor thing is probably just bored. "Satisfied, fulfilled dogs do not do this," Millan says. "If you're away most of the day, or don't play with him enough, his energy has nowhere to go. It just builds up inside him until it explodes. This could be triggered by a scent, the sight of another dog on TV, or just his own frustration."

It's not too tough to calm them down, he adds. You need to increase their activity level and tire them out. Throw a Frisbee or ball to your dog, or let him run in the park. Animals— even the most aloof—need stimulation.

Speaks gobbledygook

Dogs don't chatter, but they do whine in an almost conversational manner. It's one of the ways they communicate. If they spot a cat, they may whine to express predatory drive; if they see a dog, they might whine because they want to play. If your pooch does it while standing at your feet and adds a soft *oof* sound, he simply wants a little attention.

Drags his butt across the floor

Many a pet lover cringed in recognition after seeing the Stanley Steemer ad in which a dog rubs his bum across his owner's carpet (to her horror). This behavior, known as scooting, is sometimes caused by gastrointestinal worms or the irritation of feces-encrusted hair. But its most common source is infected or impacted anal glands.

Dogs have two large sacs inside their rectum that carry their personal scent. These usually empty when they go to the bathroom, but may become overly full of fluid or sebaceous material. They then begin to itch and the dog seeks relief by scooting.

Take affected pets to the vet or groomer. They need to have their glands expressed. It's like milking (and no, you don't want to try it at home). Beware chronic scooting with blood: It can indicate an abscess, severe inflammation or a rare cancer called anal sac adenocarcinoma.

What if your dog seems OK? The answer could be more benign. "He may simply be spreading his scent on a new environment to make it more familiar to him," says Millan. One sign he's fine: He'll scratch the ground with his nails after he rubs his rear on it. It's his way of saying, *Baby, I'm home.*

Chases his own body parts

There your dog goes again, circling around like a carousel horse, trying to grab his tail. It's amusing to watch, but it becomes less laughable when you know what's really going on. It's his cheap way of finding a toy. It usually means that he's desperate for some environmental enrichment. The Rx: the Kong (available at pet retailers like Petco and PetSmart). Stick treats or peanut butter into this rubber toy and dogs will spend many happy hours trying to ferret it out. Daily walks or games of fetch will also keep them mentally stimulated.

However, if you see your pooch biting his tail (or feet), take him to the vet. It could be a sign of itchy allergies or obsessive-compulsive disorder. Whatever you do, don't try to make him feel better by lavishing him with physical affection; it reinforces the behavior.

CARING *for* YOUR DOG

There is no substitution for taking good daily care of your dog —and the very best care is preventive. Making a daily ritual out of a few good habits results in a happy pet and significantly reduces veterinary costs later on. Regular bathing and brushing keeps your pooch sleek and minimizes trips to a professional groomer. Vigorous daily exercise and proper restraints on a walk or in the yard reduce the likelihood of injury and prevent your dog from running off. Investing in a good-quality dog food and keeping treats to a minimum will stave off those extra pounds that can compromise health. Don't wait till there's a problem to take your dog to the vet; spay or neuter at the outset and make inoculations and checkups routine.

Essential Pet Supplies for New Dog Owners

If you're a first-time dog owner, you may be wondering what pet supplies to buy. In general, there are only eight items you will need to adequately care for a dog.

1 **Dog bed** A well-crafted dog bed can provide joint support for a dog. This is especially true for older dogs. The bed should be large enough for him to spread out and stretch on. It should also contain a cushion that is of a medium firmness.

2 **Nail trimmers** Split and broken nails can be painful for a dog. As a result, you will need to trim them every four to six weeks. Do so with a nail trimmer that is specially made for the job. Most people prefer the guillotine-style nail trimmers that look like pliers. You can find them in any store that sells pet supplies. Also, when you trim your new dog's nails, avoid cutting the quick. The quick is the tender part of your dog's nail that will hurt and bleed if you cut it. You can see it easily with dogs that have white nails. For other dogs, you should conservatively cut the tip ends off the nail, about ⅛ in.

3 **Grooming brush** You should brush your dog's coat daily. Brushing helps keep his coat clean and clear of harmful debris. Wire brushes work well with medium to long or curly coats. Bristle brushes with little spacing are best for short-haired dogs. Remember, when brushing your new dog's coat, start from front to back and brush in the natural direction of the hair.

4 **Water and food bowls** Two plain, ceramic bowls are the only pet supplies you will need to adequately feed and water your new dog. However, you can go high-tech or fancy by purchasing water fountains or elevated bowls. You can even customize your dog's water and food bowls by monogramming them.

5 **Tagged collar** This is important for the safety of your new dog. If he gets lost, it will help strangers find you. Otherwise, he may end up at the pound or in the arms of another owner. Also, when purchasing a collar, be sure it isn't too tight and that you replace it as your dog grows. Your finger should easily slide between your dog's collar and neck at all times.

6 **First aid kit** In case of an emergency, you will need a first aid kit for your new dog. It should include antibiotic ointment, hydrocortisone spray or ointment, a 3cc/10cc oral medication syringe, diphenhydramine, rectal thermometer, 3 percent hydrogen peroxide, 2-in. gauze, plain saline solution, ear-cleaning solution, cotton swabs and tweezers. These items will help you address a wide range of injuries from bug bites to infections.

7 **Chew toy** This offers two-for-one benefits for a dog. Besides entertaining him, chew toys help strengthen his teeth and reduce dental problems. For puppies, make sure you purchase one that is durable and can't be broken. A puppy will be more apt to swallow a piece of it and suffer dire consequences.

8 **Leash** Many states have leash laws. These require a dog to be on a leash if he is in a public area. As a result, it is vital that you select a leash immediately for your new dog. Make sure it's long enough to allow him to walk a couple of feet ahead or to the side of you without hurting his neck.

Benefits of All-Natural Pet Supplies

What are natural pet supplies? "Natural" can mean almost anything the manufacturer wants it to mean because there are no regulations specifying what is or isn't natural. So be careful when reading labels for pet supplies you buy. Generally, natural means food, toys, supplements, bedding, etc. that are not made from synthetic ingredients or materials.

The term "organic" is often interchanged with the word natural, especially when it comes to pet food. Organic pet foods are those that are free of artificial colors, flavor enhancers, chemical additives and pesticides. They are generally made of whole grains and lean meats, and don't contain meat byproducts such as chicken fat.

The following are some of the benefits you may derive from buying all-natural pet supplies.

- **Your pet's health may improve.** Natural pet foods are more likely to provide your dog with better nutrition because your pet gets fewer chemicals and preservatives and more quality nutrients and vitamins. Many dogs that suffer from skin allergies often get better when switched from regular commercial pet foods to organic or natural pet foods. Because natural pet foods are made from leaner meats and whole grains (instead of simple, more sugary carbohydrates), your pet may be less likely to become obese. Obesity can lead to complications such as diabetes and arthritis.

- **Natural products may be safer for your children.** Because natural products don't contain harsh or toxic chemicals, they may be less harmful if your child accidentally gets into them.

- **You'll help protect the environment.** Most natural products are made with the environment in mind, whether it's the product itself or the container it comes in. Often, natural products break down and are absorbed more easily into the environment than the chemical agents that are used to make up less natural products.

- **Your pet may be more comfortable wearing natural collars and leashes.** The standard nylon collar is made to last, not to give your dog comfortable protection. Try a more natural fiber instead, such as hemp webbing, which is durable but comfortable because it softens over time.

It's important to remember that not all natural products are perfect, just as not all less natural products are bad. When determining what's best for your dog, especially when it comes to diet, always consult your veterinarian, who is usually familiar with a wide variety of products.

10 Reasons to Use All-Natural Pet Care Products

Just as you wouldn't use harsh chemicals on a newborn baby, you should also try to avoid chemical-packed pet care products. Fortunately, as people move toward earth-friendly and natural goods, more and more all-natural pet products find their way to market. Choosing to go all-natural for your pet may reduce your overall pet care product choices, but what you do end up using will be much better for your best friend. Here are some of the many benefits of switching to all-natural pet products.

1 **Natural products have a proven track record.** Many forget that chemical and synthetic products are somewhat new arrivals on the shelves of markets and pet stores. Natural remedies, on the other hand, have been around for centuries and are time-proven solutions to common maladies facing your pet.

2 **Natural products are good for the environment.** Chemicals eventually make their way back into our water supply, our air and our soil, thus damaging our planet and wildlife. Our pets interact daily with the planet, and when the environment is chemical-laden, expect your pets to ingest chemicals, too. Natural products do not have these nasty environmental side effects.

3 **Synthetic compounds can damage an animal's skin and fur.** Natural flea and tick remedies, on the other hand, have essential oils that benefit an animal's coat and skin while ridding your pet of fleas and ticks.

4 **Pesticides used in pet shampoos can trigger adverse reactions in many animals.** These range from simple allergic reactions to premature death. Avoid these pesticides, choose natural, and know that your pet is safer.

5 **Natural products are often handmade with care.** The quality of handmade products often surpasses the quality of industrially made ones.

6 **Certain chemicals used on pets are not meant to be ingested.** But just like children, animals swallow, chew and lick just about anything, including those poisonous chemicals. Opting for natural pet care products will ensure your pet's health and safety.

7 **Synthetic products affect our bodies as well as those of our pets.** Natural products leave our air clean and our bodies happy.

8 **Natural products are often made by local boutique stores.** Synthetic products, on the other hand, are made by large chemical plants. By supporting all-natural products, you are supporting small local businesses.

9 **Most all-natural products are not tested on animals.** Pet owners can agree that this is an important attribute of all-natural supplies.

10 **Synthetic pet products often provoke more allergies in animals.** This is due to the many additives used. Pets are less likely to experience allergic reactions to natural products, so you can feel at ease when applying them to your best friend.

56

Earth-Friendly Pet Supplies

We all love our pets, but shouldn't we love our environment just as much? Thanks to the green revolution and the ensuing availability of more earth-friendly pet supplies, we can love our pets and Mother Nature without favoring one over the other.

- **Go fetch!** Zisc is the newest in a line of flying discs. Keep your canine well exercised and entertained with this fun toy. It's made out of a material called Zogoflex, which is completely safe for your dog and the earth. Zisc is so durable that if your pup manages to damage it, it will be replaced for free. Zisc is also entirely dishwasher safe and recyclable. Zisc; *westpawdesign.com*

- **One-two-three eliminate** As much as loving owners don't mind picking up their dog's doo-doo, the waste it generates does contribute to the environment's pollution problem. (Think of all the plastic bags used!) Now you can eliminate your dog's waste in a safe and smell-free way. The Doggie Poo Eliminator is an amazingly easy way to dispose of your furry friend's waste right in your backyard. The waste will be broken down by bacteria in the composter while the excess liquid gets soaked into the ground. Doggie Poo Eliminator; *composters.com*

- **Tug-of-war** Decimating tug toys is often a favorite activity of puppies as well as adult dogs. Hemp rope toys are ideal for pooches that love to chew, and they're easy on the Earth, too. These hemp rope toys are durable and made entirely of Romanian hemp. Plus, 10 percent of proceeds go toward pro-pet programs. Hemp rope toys; *earthdog.com*

57

Best Pet Supplies for Cleaning Up Pet Messes

We love our pets, but we could do very well without the offensive messes, smells and stains they often leave behind. Some odors, like that of urine, can last forever in a spot if you don't take care of it right away. Fortunately, there are many pet supplies on the market today that can help remove the results of a pet accident from your favorite carpet or couch.

- **Bounty paper towels** This is your first defense against vomit, feces and urine messes. Place a couple of these towels over the pile, press gently with your shoe and allow the towel to absorb most of the mess. (With firm feces, you can use the towel to pick up the mess without soiling your hands.) The next step is to use a stain and odor remover.

- **Nature's Miracle Stain and Odor Remover** This product works by using natural enzymes to break down organic stains and odors such as those left by vomit, feces and urine. The manufacturer claims that because of its natural ingredients, it's safer to use than products with harsher chemicals, guaranteeing that it's nontoxic, nonflammable and safe on colors and all water-safe surfaces. For removing stains from carpets, clothes and furniture, Nature's Miracle comes in liquid, spray and detergent forms, starting at $5.75 for a 32-oz bottle. It also eliminates urine odors, increasing the chances that your pet won't be lured

back to the same spot again to urinate. Enzymatic products are often inactivated by certain chemicals. If using an enzymatic cleaner, don't combine it with another product unless specifically directed by the manufacturer. Check out *petsnmore.com* for more information.

- **Urine Finder UV Fluorescent Tube** Want to add a high-tech flair to your pet cleaning? Try the battery-operated UV Fluorescent Tube, which helps you identify the exact locations of dried urine to eliminate old urine odors at their source. Cost: $9.95 at *superhappypets.com*

- **Vinegar** If you're the do-it-yourself type, you may find that some of the best pet products are in your own cupboards or drawers. For new pet stains, remove them with a quart of warm water, ½ cup of white vinegar and several white paper towels.

Remember, the best way to deal with pet messes is to prevent them from happening in the first place. Make sure you take your dog out in time to avoid accidents in your home.

Pet-Proof Your House

🐾 **Plants** If your pet gets into your lilies, azaleas or philodendron, it can spell bad news. All are toxic to dogs and cats, so place potted ones out of reach and keep an eye on your pet when he's in the yard. Also, never use cocoa mulch—it contains caffeine and theobromine, both of which can be deadly to dogs. For a complete list of dangerous plants, go to *thepetshow.com* and click on "Pet Tips."

🐾 **Chew toys** Before you give your dog that rawhide bone, make sure it's American-made. Imported rawhide can be contaminated with salmonella or chemicals.

Pet Financials 101: Have Pet, Will Pay

Look at that face! The moment potential pet owners lay eyes on a sweet little puppy, they're goners. But in the rush of emotion that comes with pet adoption, few consider the long-term costs, which can be at least $400 or more annually, according to the ASPCA. The good news: It's surprisingly easy to save money on pet care. Just follow these insider tips.

Vet Care

When deciding on a pet, choose a mixed breed that has been reared by a friend, reliable breeder or trusted shelter. Hybrid animals tend to be hardier than purebreds, who often have hereditary diseases, or those from pet stores, who may have acquired illnesses in animal mills. Lower costs further by adopting pets over a year old; they'll likely have been spayed or neutered, and had shots and training.

Next, spend a little to save a lot. The biggest mistake owners make is not keeping up with routine preventive care. People forgo $15 vaccines, then their pets get $2,000 infections. Never skip core vaccinations, annual checkups, flea-and-tick treatments, heartworm drugs, or spaying/neutering—they save thousands down the line. Swiping wet gauze or a pet toothbrush over your animal's teeth daily will even help stave off serious disease.

Slash nonessentials. Call vets with minor questions (rather than visiting) and ask about package deals for treating several pets. Teaching hospitals, shelters and branches of The Humane Society offer cheap treatments, but weigh those savings against quality of care. If your pet needs multiple procedures, double-book surgeries: You'll pay just once for anesthetic and hospital stays.

Finally, if you smoke, quit. Pets suffer severely from secondhand smoke. They ingest the particles that settle on their fur and can develop asthma, lymphoma, bronchitis and lung cancer.

Food

Nothing siphons cash faster than feeding your pets gourmet or premium food, which can cost $5 a can or $50 a bag. You may think you're treating them well, but the truth is, pets don't need it. Just look for a well-known, high-quality brand name, and buy it in bulk at a discount store. You'll slash costs by a third. Don't go too cheap, though: Generic and local brands may not have the same level of nutritional research.

If your pet is overweight, like 35% of those in the U.S., a simple measuring cup can mean more money for you and fewer pounds for him. Use it to dole out the correct portion, based on the package's feeding recommendations.

Also, ask your vet which of your food picks have the most "bioavailable" nutrients; these meet pets' nutritional needs faster and keep them from overeating. Give them high-protein foods and they'll be satisfied sooner.

Grooming

Professional grooming isn't just a way to keep your pet looking good; it also prevents medical problems from developing. But shelling out up to $100 every month can be tough. Slash costs by keeping pets in good condition before bringing them in.

Go over your pet's fur with a wire-bristled slicker brush, and then follow up with a double-sided stainless steel comb (like the Greyhound, $17; *afortunatedog.com*) once or twice a week, making sure to thoroughly penetrate the fur from root to topcoat. Matted hair is the biggest bugaboo in grooming. Also, bathe dogs with hypoallergenic pet shampoo. You can lengthen the time between visits by requesting a "puppy" or "lion" trim: Fur is shorn as short as half an inch, which means fewer grooming sessions. Animals like it, too. They love really feeling your hand when you pet them.

To keep expenses down even more, do touchups at home. Grooming schools offer in-depth courses (*petgroomer.com*), but a quick, inexpensive lesson from a groomer, vet or certified pet stylist should cover the basics. For dog owners, check out champion groomer Jodi Murphy's how-to videos (*jodimurphy.net*). You can find the tools you'll need, like fur clippers and nail clipper-styptic sets, at most big-box stores. While DIY may set you back a few bucks in the short term, you'll save hundreds in the long run. Prefer leaving it to the pros? Ask if groomers offer discounts to clients who rebook frequently.

Toys

Buying a bushel of gadgets to entertain pets is like getting a flat-screen TV just to watch *Law & Order*: awesome, but unnecessary. People really overspend on pet toys. They'll give a 5-pound dog 25 pounds of stuff. Truth is, pets prefer basic toys and are more likely to play with an empty box than with a $20 animatronic mouse.

Huge hunks of plain, U.S.-made rawhide are perfect (imported versions may contain contaminants). Give them three of those, and they'll be happy. Many teeth have been broken by harder nylon toys and too many sock toys have been removed from dogs' intestines to recommend them. Another good option: the Kong, an indestructible rubber ball that you can stuff with food. It will keep your dog happily occupied for hours.

Cut the Cost of Pet Care

So how can you afford to care for your furry friend—in sickness and in health? Make preventive maintenance your top priority as a pet owner and you'll save later on.

Basics

- **Restrain them.** A fence or some other reasonable restraint is the best way to avoid big vet bills. Dogs should always be leashed, fenced or supervised.

- **Choose the right food.** Skip all the fancy premium foods sold by vets. Use name-brand pet food from the supermarket labeled "complete and balanced." Or look for the seal of approval of AAFCO (the Association of American Feed Control Officials). Stick with the same brand. Switching abruptly can cause health issues for some animals. And less is better, as slightly underweight pets have fewer health problems.

- **Spay and neuter.** Reproductive issues aside, spayed and neutered dogs have fewer health and behavioral problems.

Keep Them Healthy

- **Make wellness routine.** Some pet supply stores offer in-store clinics and special events. Humane societies and veterinary schools offer low-cost clinics where inoculations and wellness exams are administered by professionals. Keep good records of the inoculations and treatments your pet has had.

- **Anticipate future medical bills.** Instead of sending premiums to an insurance company, consider putting the amount you'd pay in premiums into a savings account.

- **Consider prepaid.** Enroll in the discount wellness plan offered by Banfield, The Pet Hospital (*banfield.net*), a national chain of pet care facilities. You pay a set fee each month so that all of the wellness exams and inoculations are covered. With enrollment comes deeply discounted office visits and services should they be necessary.

- **Go for second opinions.** Even if it's an emergency, if the estimate is for more than a few hundred dollars, get a second opinion. If the estimate is for $800 and you can only afford $400, speak up. There may be less aggressive and cheaper alternative treatments.

- **Shop around for medications.** Ask your vet for prescription drug samples to get started. Then call around to retailers such as Walmart or Costco pharmacies (many meds are the same for humans and animals) to compare prices. Search websites like *discountpetmedicines.com* or *1800petmeds.com*, too.

Do You Need Pet Health Insurance?

Pet owners today who value their pet's health generally consider pet insurance a good idea. Because medicine has improved dramatically over the past several years, it is possible to provide a very high level of care for your pet. Because there are very expensive procedures performed on dogs, pet insurance can provide peace of mind for pet owners. Pet insurance can also be the right and responsible move if you are bringing a new pet home.

- **Health coverage** Having a pet insurance plan will provide a range of coverage, depending on how much you pay into it per month. Having pet insurance provides assistance for large and unmanageable health bills that may occur. Many pets will need emergency care as a result of unforeseen circumstances, and preventive health care coverage and maintenance coverage can make having a health plan for your pet an easy decision.

- **Financing pet health treatments** If your pet has genetic conditions or a chronic disease, having pet insurance will allow you to provide a high level of care for your pet while controlling expenses. This is much better than having to pay the entire cost upfront, and repeatedly, based on the number of office visits you need to make. By opting for pet insurance, you'll not only get to pay dues in installments, but also much of the cost above the annual deductible will be reimbursed.

- **Insurance can cover wellness** You can purchase an additional wellness plan on top of your standard insurance to cover routine checkups, dental cleanings and exams, blood panels, microchip installation, spaying and neutering, and other common procedures. Because most pet insurance providers operate in a manner similar to a PPO, you will pay the costs of pet health upfront and then be reimbursed by the insurance provider. You will be happy with a wellness plan because it generally pays for itself.

- **Insurance can cover prescription medications** Prescription medications for animals can be very expensive to purchase without insurance. Having an insurance plan takes away this expense and makes it either free or extremely affordable, depending on the plan you purchase. Older animals may need prescription medications regularly to maintain pet health, and animals with genetic problems take medications often.

Pet insurance can be an essential part of providing for your pet's well-being. Ensure that you get the right plan for your pet by comparing plan services and deductibles before making a decision.

Affordable Pet Health Insurance: Does It Exist?

If you've taken your pet to the veterinarian recently, you know that the bills can add up quickly. Shots, preventive care, injury treatment and other services increase in price every year, so it makes sense to consider pet health insurance. The question, though, is whether affordable options exist.

- **Types of insurance companies** There are many ways you can provide your pet with health insurance, and the type of insurance company you choose will have a direct impact on what you pay. In many cases, insuring a pet with a major provider will yield tremendous savings. For example, an insurance company that is affiliated with a major organization such as the ASPCA or the PurinaCare insurance programs has a larger customer base and therefore more flexibility. If you go with a smaller company such as a local provider, you might wind up paying more.

- **Mitigating insurance costs** Most people know that if they have an alarm or an antilock brake system installed on their vehicle, they will pay less for auto insurance. The same concept applies to pet insurance, but in a different way. You'll pay less if your pet has reduced risk factors for potential emergencies. If your pet is not yet implanted with a microchip, for instance, it might be a good time to have it done. A microchip is a tiny device that is injected between your pet's shoulder blades. Should your pet wander off or be stolen from your yard, the microchip can be scanned when the pet is found, and positively identified. Most pet health insurance companies offer a discount for microchipped pets.

- **Multiple pet discounts** You can also save money on insurance if all of your pets are covered under the same policy. The same is true if you purchase other types of insurance from the same company. For example, many equine insurance companies offer both liability insurance and health insurance to horse owners, which can reduce the overall cost.

- **Coverage levels** Another way to find affordable pet health insurance is to evaluate the different coverage levels provided by insurance companies. Some policies cover everything from preventive care to emergency surgery, while others have restrictions related to procedures and treatment options. Premiums can range anywhere from $10 to more than $100 per month, depending on the level of coverage. The more expensive options will cover a larger percentage of each procedure (up to 100 percent, in some cases), while cheaper options will mean paying more out of pocket when you take your pet to the vet.

- **The bottom line** Insurance for your pet may seem expensive at first, but compared with what pet owners might have to pay out of pocket for veterinary expenses, it is actually just a drop in the bucket. It is possible to save thousands of dollars if your pet is adequately insured.

When you go shopping for insurance, make sure to get the policy details spelled out right away. What treatments are covered? In what circumstances will claims be rejected? Do premiums increase as your pet ages? Knowing the answers to these questions will help you find an affordable solution that will still protect your animal friend.

Tips for Choosing a Dog Sitter

When you and your family want to get away for the weekend, you want to know your pet is in good hands. Choosing a dog sitter is often preferable to putting your dog in a kennel, but how do you go about finding the right chaperone for your canine companion? Below, find some helpful tips for choosing a pet sitter.

- **Ask for references.** Before you consider hiring a dog sitter, ask for three to five personal and professional references. This will ensure someone else has hired and been satisfied with the sitter and her work. It also is a good idea to request that no references be direct relatives. Of course, there will be times when you meet a dog sitter who is looking for her first job. In cases such as these, spend time with the sitter before you go on vacation to watch how she interacts with your dog. If no red flags pop up, you're probably safe.

- **Meet the sitter.** If you find your dog sitter online or via a referral, be sure to meet her before taking off for your vacation and get to know her as best you can to ensure quality pet care. This also will allow you to use your instincts to judge her character and abilities. Ideally, you should meet at home when choosing a dog sitter. This way, she will have a chance to meet your dog and the rest of your family, which can eliminate territorial issues. You also will get a chance to see the professional interact with your dog.

- **Ask about memberships.** If you really want to be careful about pet care, ask the sitter if she belongs to any professional organizations. The National Association of Professional Pet Sitters, for example, has important guidelines to protect pet owners and is a great resource for finding a qualified sitter. The professional you hire does not necessarily have to be associated with such an organization, but it definitely helps. It means that she is serious about her work and committed to following industry guidelines.

- **Compare prices.** Money may be no object when it comes to pet care in your family, but don't overpay for a qualified sitter. Ask upfront how much the professional charges. Find out if there are any additional fees such as mileage for traveling to your house or extra charges for walking your dog.

- **Ask probing questions.** Sometimes the best strategy is to play the "what if" game with a potential sitter. Ask a series of questions about potential situations and how the sitter would handle them. For example, what if she gets sick and can't make it one day? What if you get stuck and can't get home when you said you would? What if your dog becomes ill or injured?

While-You're-Away Pet Care Checklist

When you must leave home without your dog, you need to provide more pet care than someone merely coming to fill the food bowl. Here is a checklist for what needs to be done before you go.

- ❀ **Have your pet meet her sitter in advance.** Always arrange a meeting with the pet sitter and your animal before you leave town, especially when it's the first time you're using this person. This increases the chances that your dog will be comfortable with the pet sitter, and that you can fully discuss your pet's needs.

- ❀ **Nail down your departure and arrival times with the sitter.** If there are any changes while you're away, call your sitter right away, especially if your trip takes longer than expected or you miss a flight home.

- ❀ **Leave all your phone numbers with the sitter.** Do this even if you think your sitter already has them. Leave your home and cell phone numbers, your veterinarian's number and the phone number of someone who can fill in for you in case you can't be reached.

- ❀ **Decide beforehand how often you want to speak with the sitter.** If you want to call for a moment every day, let the sitter know. Don't be embarrassed to express your need for reassurance that your dog is doing OK in your absence.

- ❀ **Don't forget to give your sitter your house key.** Also, tell your sitter who else has your key—and their phone numbers—in case the sitter loses the key.

- ❀ **Make sure your pet's ID information is up-to-date.** This includes tags, microchips, etc. This will be infinitely helpful in case your pet gets lost. This is one of the most important aspects of pet care.

- ❀ **Tell your sitter if your pet is not allowed somewhere in the house.** This can mean anything from the basement or the kitchen to the bed or sofa. Pets can be quite clever at trying to get away with something when their owner isn't there to scold them.

- ❀ **Write a complete list of everything your pet needs.** This includes: » Food and where it's kept, and how much and how often your pet is fed. » Medicines, including where they're kept and written instructions on how they're administered. » Your pet's favorite toys. » Your dog's leash, harness and walking routine. » Any places your dog shouldn't walk, such as any places he may be afraid of or overly aggressive in. » Whether any other animals are allowed near your pet.

- ❀ **Leave a copy of your pet's medical records.** Also leave the name and number of an emergency veterinary hospital you would use if your regular veterinarian is not available.

- ❀ **Leave a signed and dated note giving permission for your sitter to take your pet to your veterinarian in an emergency.** Discuss beforehand under what circumstances you want to be notified first and what constitutes a real emergency in which your sitter should take your pet off to the vet immediately. And—this is very important—discuss how you will pay for emergency veterinary care. Some animal hospitals won't treat an animal unless they have a credit card number to bill or receive advance payment.

Traveling with Your Pet: 5 Essential Pet Health Records

Before you pack up your car for a summer road trip with your dog, be sure your pet's health records are handy. These important documents will prove vital in the face of travel-related health hazards, such as increased exposure to fleas and ticks, a medical emergency or an unexplained illness. Here is what your pet health records should include:

1 **Provide your veterinarian's contact information.** The first page of your records should include your veterinarian's name, address, phone number, e-mail address and fax number. This information will come in handy if you need immediate advice on how to treat an injury or if another vet needs more information on your pet's medical history.

2 **Keep records on shots and vaccinations.** If your pet is exposed to a dangerous disease during travel, you must inform the treating vet of his shots and vaccinations—difficult details to remember, especially in an emergency. Have a copy of your pet's documented shot and vaccination history. This information will give the vet an overview of your pet's health and help him decide how to treat him.

3 **Supply written prescriptions for medications.** Does your pet take a daily medication to control an illness or condition? If so, don't forget to bring a copy of the written prescription with you on the road. Medication can get lost in the shuffle during travel, so you may need to get a refill. Imagine how your trip will be ruined if this isn't possible.

4 **Document past medical emergencies.** List your pet's past medical emergencies, and keep them with his health records. Provide the attending vet information on visits that required surgery, long-term medication or a change in lifestyle so he can make appropriate care decisions based on your pet's medical history.

5 **Discuss current diet and allergic reactions.** Does your pet suffer from allergies or swell up if he eats chicken? You need to list this type of information in your pet's health records. It is particularly helpful when you stay in a five-star hotel and hotel staff is planning the menu for your pet. Those people need to know what not to feed your pet so he stays healthy.

Keeping these five vital pet health documents handy is essential for the well-being of your dog as he travels. Be sure to keep all original documents at home and put a copy in a packet or folder that you can take with you. With luck, you will never need to use any of this information, but if you do, you'll be adequately prepared.

Pet Care 101: Summer Care Tips

Summertime means fun in the sun for you and your family. However, summer days can be dangerous or even fatal for your dog if you don't provide the proper pet care. Here are a few steps to take to ensure your canine companion has a safe, fun-filled summer.

- **Avoid heat stroke.** All pets are susceptible to heat stroke in the summer. However, dogs are at a heightened risk because they tend to be outdoors more often. Heat stroke occurs when your dog has an abnormally high body temperature that may lead to organ failure or even death. Dogs don't perspire; they release body heat by panting and through the pads of their feet, so they have a harder time cooling down. Limit their time outdoors and never leave them in a car—it can reach over 100 degrees in minutes. Make sure they have plenty of shade and fresh water, and keep your home cool. Be careful with snub-nosed breeds (bulldogs, Boston terriers and pugs); they have a harder time panting. If your pet displays signs of heat stress—heavy panting, glazed eyes, lethargy, rapid heartbeat, discolored tongue, and even unconsciousness—lower his body temperature immediately by applying cool, wet towels, and call your vet.

- **Follow outdoor safety guidelines.** If you leave your dog outdoors, be sure that the area has protection from the sun. Your dog requires shade on hot summer days to avoid heat stroke. You can plant shade trees or large shrubs to provide natural sun protection for your canine buddy. Dogs love to roll around on the lawn, and the grass can help cool your pet down on hot afternoons. Be sure that your dog has access to a nice grassy patch. Keep water bowls filled. You may want to consider providing an extra bowl or two of water on hot summer days. Have your children help by checking the dog's water every day.

- **Prevent sunburn.** Like their owners, animals can also get a sunburn. And light-colored dogs are at special risk for skin cancer. To keep burns at bay, apply pet-safe SPF 15 or 40 sunscreen (found at pet stores) to the bridge of your dog's nose and to the tips of the ears.

Outdoor poisons

Fertilizers, herbicides and insecticides All three of these common garden products can spell disaster if pets chew into the packages. Insecticides in particular can be fatal if eaten. Store concentrated products somewhere inaccessible to pets. If your pet ingests toxins, call Animal Poison Control immediately (888-426-4435). If he's gasping or seizing, rush him to the vet.

Pet Care 101: Winter Care Tips

When the temperatures start to drop and snow begins to pile up, your dog feels the difference just as much as you do. Although dogs are naturally equipped to withstand extreme temperatures, winterizing your dogs can make a world of difference, both to them and to you.

- **Leash up.** Your dog might think it's a great idea to run loose around your neighborhood after a snowstorm, but don't let those adorable eyes taint your judgment. According to the ASPCA, loose dogs can lose familiar scents in the snow and easily become lost.

- **Watch the weather.** Outdoor dogs will probably be fine for most of the winter in milder climates, but if the temperatures start to dip below freezing, make other arrangements. You can provide a sheltered area outdoors with blankets to keep your dog warm, or you can bring him inside your home or garage.

- **Know your toxins.** Certain lethal poisons build up during the winter, threatening to trump your other pet care efforts. Salt, for example, is lethal to dogs if ingested in large amounts, and your pet might be tempted to run his tongue along salted streets when out for a walk. Similarly, antifreeze that leaks from your car is also poisonous, so make sure you mop up any spills immediately (see box below).

- **Let it grow.** Your dog's coat is a natural protective shield against cold weather, so don't shave it during the winter months. In fact, it is a good idea to let summer coats start growing out in early fall so they are prepared for the onset of frigid temperatures.

- **Get trendy.** You may laugh when you see people carrying around their dogs in T-shirts and other fancy pet clothes. However, this serves a valuable purpose in winter, particularly for short-haired breeds. A sweater or even a cotton T-shirt—type garment is perfect for dogs in areas where temperatures are particularly cold.

- **Feel the breeze.** Windchill can make a cold winter day almost unbearable, so consider your dog when making plans. If the wind is strong or particularly cold, keep your dog inside and away from drafts. On these days, it is usually also best to forget the afternoon walk. If your home is particularly drafty, make sure he has a place to sleep off the floor so he isn't chilled.

- **Wipe the paws.** When your dog comes in from playing in the backyard, he might bring with him clumps of ice or snow on his paws. This is especially true of long-haired canines, whose fur around the paws grows especially long. When your dog is ready to come back inside, wipe his paws and underbelly with a towel.

- **Check the pads.** Even if you are diligent with the towel, your dog's paws might start to crack and bleed during the winter. You can add a touch of petroleum jelly to his paws as part of your normal pet care regimen, which will help seal the cracks and prevent infection.

Outdoor poisons

Antifreeze This substance tastes sweet to animals, yet it's anything but. Kidney failure can develop within hours of ingesting it. Use less toxic antifreeze made with propylene glycol, not ethylene glycol (the label says "dog-safe"); store it securely and watch for car leaks. If your pet ingests antifreeze, take him to the vet right away.

Must-Have Pet Supplies for Grooming Your Dog

Providing proper care for your dog through quality pet products is a worthwhile investment in giving her a long, healthy and happy life. Leave your house fur-free and reward your pooch with a great lifestyle by checking out these effective products.

- **Peppermint conditioning shampoo** Ditch those popular harsh and abrasive pet shampoos in favor of this all-natural peppermint conditioning shampoo. This product uses essential oils such as peppermint and tea tree to clean and soothe your pup. The essential oils produce a clean and fresh scent and provide natural flea control. Peppermint conditioning shampoo, $12.99 for 16 oz; *dog.com*

- **Animals Apawthecary Herbal Ear Rinse** This herbal ear rinse for dogs makes the otherwise unpleasant task of cleaning a dog's ears a calming experience for your pup. This safe, chemical-free product contains healthy ingredients such as aloe vera, witch hazel and olive leaf. Animals Apawthecary Herbal Ear Rinse, $9.71 for 4 oz; *springvalleyherbs.com*

- **U Groom 7-Piece Dog Grooming Kit** This kit has it all, and fits everything into one compact box—perfect for traveling and easy storage. This essential grooming pet-supply kit contains slicker brush, rake, comb, flea comb, hair scissor, nail file and nail clippers. U Groom 7pc Dog Grooming Kit, $29.99; *pawpalaceonline.com*

- **Soap on a Rope** Keep your dog's coat healthy with Soap on a Rope. This soap consists of natural vegetable and essential oils, contains no harsh chemicals and will leave your dog feeling clean. Soap on a Rope, $10; *pawprintzpetboutique.com*

- **FURminator deShedding Tool** This little device has been hailed by pet owners for its gentle and precise de-shedding ability. The FURminator is designed to reduce your dog's undercoat (the main shedding culprit) but leave the shiny topcoat intact. FURminator deShedding Tool, $34.95 small, $49.95 medium, $59.95 large; *petsmart.com*

- **Metrovac Air Force QuickDraw Dryer** Getting a thick-coated dog dry after a bath is essential to preserving a dry home! With this dryer, you can prevent that problem and give your dog a more comfortable grooming experience. Metrovac Air Force QuickDraw Dryer, $99.99; *petsmart.com*

Pet Care 101: Grooming Your Dog

Tired of matted fur, smelly dog breath and dirt tracked throughout your house? One of the most crucial aspects of pet care is grooming your dog, both for the animal and for the people living in your home. Of course, dogs are fond of digging in the yard, rolling in mud and sticking their nose in the trash, so how do you keep your four-legged friend as clean as possible?

- **Routine grooming** The easiest way to groom your dog is to set up a schedule. If you do it once or twice a week, each session will take less time and you won't have to worry about him making a mess in the house. This might be a chore that family members can share: Mom takes care of it on Mondays, Dad on Thursdays, and so on. Some dogs love to be groomed; others would rather visit the "v-e-t." To make it easier on yourself and your pet, set up a specific time and place for grooming.

- **Brush options** Some pet owners use regular hairbrushes on their dogs, and this can work for certain breeds. However, it helps to use tools that are specifically recommended for animals. The FURminator, for example, is highly recommended for dogs that tend to shed, and is designed to remove as much loose hair as possible. Ideally, you want a brush that won't hurt your dog's skin but will separate the hairs and leave them smooth and shiny. Try a variety of brushes, and switch to a soft brush for smoothing the coat at the end of grooming.

- **Start at the top** Grooming your dog should be a top-to-bottom exercise. Begin with your dog's head and work slowly down to his tail with a brush, making sure to hit the hard-to-reach areas like his chest and abdomen. Spend extra time on areas where the undercoat tends to flourish, such as the back and the sides of the legs. Long-haired dogs will need a brush with metal bristles that separate those long hairs and remove clumps of undercoat. You can use a softer brush on short-haired dogs or animals with sensitive skin. Make sure to pay attention to your dog's reaction; if the brushing seems to be painful, let up on the pressure.

- **Clipping the nails** Your dog's nails are another essential part of pet care, as long nails can snag on carpet and grass and scratch human legs. They are also unkind to furniture if your dog prefers the couch to his doggy bed. If you are worried about accidentally cutting a vein, you can grind your dog's nails instead of clipping them. You can find cordless grinders that allow you to work outside, and the machine will grind down the nail without danger to your dog's paws. (See next page for more on nails.)

- **Eliminating doggy breath** If your dog breathes a wisp of green smoke every time he exhales, it might be time to start focusing on dental pet care. Brushing your dog's teeth every three months or so will help prevent decay and keep his teeth healthy. There are specially formulated brushes and toothpastes that work wonders with dog mouths.

Safety tips

- Never brush your dog's teeth without first putting your fingers in his mouth to get him used to the sensation. Otherwise, he might instinctively bite down.

- Have someone else hold your dog's head the first time you clip or grind his nails. This way, you'll be protected if he decides he doesn't like the feeling.

- Bathe your dog only once every month or so. Frequent bathing can lead to dry skin and irritation, so stick with grooming most of the time.

Pet Care 101: Clipping Your Dog's Nails

If you are a dog owner, you eventually must trim your dog's nails as part of your regular pet care routine. Unlike cats, dogs cannot retract their nails, and without regular clipping, a dog's nails will grow toward its paw pads and cause pain. If you hear a clicking noise while walking your dog, it's time to trim its nails.

You may have a dog that requires only an occasional nail trim. Some dogs keep their nails consistently short and naturally file them by walking, running and playing.

However, if your dog's nails continue to grow, you'll need to learn how to trim the nails or pay for the service at your local veterinarian, dog groomer or other pet care professional.

- **Watch an expert.** If you never have clipped your dog's nails, take your dog to your veterinarian for a lesson. The vet can show you how to clip the nails without hurting the quick—the portion of the nail containing nerves and blood vessels. Your vet also can show you the most effective way to hold the dog down during the process.

- **Purchase a quality nail clipper.** Once you have learned how to clip your dog's nails, you should purchase a quality nail clipper. According to the College of Veterinary Medicine at Washington State University, the best nail clipper for dogs is the guillotine type. With these clippers, you simply place the dog's nail into the ring and squeeze the trigger to cut it. You can find a guillotine-style dog nail trimmer at your local pet store, or you can purchase a colored trimmer, complete with nail file and styptic dispenser.

- **Get a helper.** As with many pet care procedures, many dogs do not like having their nails trimmed. Your dog may or may not tolerate the process. Hold down your dog, and begin trimming the first nail. If your dog resists, recruit a helper. If you have another person who can help hold the dog still, you can focus on trimming the dog's nails, and you will be less likely to hit the quick.

- **First-time clipper:** When you use the clipper for the first time, start by removing small pieces of the dog's nail. If your dog has black nails, taking small cuts is particularly important as you will not be able to see the quick. If your dog has lighter-colored nails, you can see the quick as the light penetrates the nail. Cut the nail close to the quick, about 2 mm or $\frac{1}{16}$ in. from it.

Keep a styptic pencil or dispenser on hand to stop your dog's bleeding in case you accidentally cut the quick. As you become more experienced with trimming your dog's nails, the entire process will be faster, and you'll know when to stop cutting to avoid hitting the quick.

Dog Food FAQs

Selecting the right dog food for your pet can be complicated. Do you choose food made with beef, fish, chicken or go vegan? Should you make your own pet food at home?

Every dog owner has to make some important decisions when it comes to feeding his or her pet, so it's a good idea to do some research to make the most informed choices. Here are some of the most frequently asked questions about dog food and your pet's nutrition:

Don't dogs get bored eating the same food every day?
Most dogs really don't have a problem eating the same food every day, but you can change things up a bit by rotating different flavors or textures of food throughout the week. Still, most dogs will be just fine eating the same meal day in, day out.

How much protein does my dog really need?
Many pet food brands tout the percentage of protein in each serving by posting the information right on the front of the package. According to the Association of American Feed Control Officials, the average adult dog needs to eat a diet comprised of about 18 percent protein; growing puppies need about 22 percent. As long as you're within this range, your dog should not be suffering from any type of protein deficiency.

How should I switch foods for my dog?
If your dog is showing signs of a food intolerance or food allergy, you will need to phase out the problem food slowly. Mixing the old and new food together for about a week is the best way to ensure that your dog will take to the new food easily.

What foods are poisonous to dogs?
Dogs should not be fed the following: chocolate, grapes and raisins, organ meats such as liver, macadamia nuts, onions, garlic, any type of dairy products or caffeine. All of these foods can cause problems for your dog; she will likely need to see a vet after consuming them.

Does my dog need to be on a weight-loss diet?
Experts say that a dog that is over 15 percent of his or her ideal body weight is obese and must start losing weight gradually. You will need to reduce the amount of calories your dog consumes each day, and limit the amount of treats and snacks, too. Making sure your dog is physically active with walks, games or running at a steady pace at least once or twice a day will also help her maintain a healthy weight.

Choosing the best dog food for your pet can take some time and research, but you need to take steps to see that your dog is eating a well-balanced diet on a regular basis. A healthy diet ensures your dog will have plenty of energy, and that she will stay healthy and strong for the years ahead.

10 Tips for Choosing a Dog Food

You worry about what goes into your body, so it only makes sense to be concerned about what food goes into your dog's body, too. There is an overwhelming array of dog foods to choose from, and yes, there is a difference between them.

Here are 10 tips for choosing a dog food that is just right for you and your pet.

1 **Age** The age of your pet is a factor in what food you buy for him. As your dog grows older, he will need different food and different amounts of it. Many brands have separate products intended for puppies and for "seniors." You should generally feed your dog puppy food until he has reached his adult size. This happens around 9 months old for a dog under 20 pounds, and around 12 to 14 months for medium-size dogs. Very large dogs may not reach their full size until they are 2 years old. Between the ages of 5 and 7, you can start feeding your dog senior food, which will meet his changing dietary needs.

2 **Quality of ingredients** If you care about high-quality ingredients in your own food, why not keep quality in mind when choosing a dog food? Higher quality may be reflected in prices, but beware of name brands that charge more simply because they're well known. Instead, ask your vet which foods he recommends. Look for foods that list a specific type of meat, such as turkey or chicken, among the first ingredients.

3 **Byproducts** Some dog foods include animal byproducts, which are the parts of animals that cannot be used in human food, such as bones and fur. At the very least, these foods can make your dog smell. At worst, they can cause digestive and other health issues, shortening your dog's lifespan. Check for foods that are labeled free of byproducts and read the ingredient list carefully. If the term "meal" is listed, pick a different food. "Meal" is a term for a random mixture of ground-up animal parts. Foods marked as "organic" or "natural" do not use byproducts.

4 **Odor** If you have issues with odor—either with the odor of your dog's food or his breath—you might want to make odor avoidance a priority when choosing dog food. Digestive issues are a common cause of bad breath in dogs, so choosing all-natural foods may fix the problem. Wet foods might also make your dog's breath smell, so try to choose a dry food.

5 **Breed** Some breeds may benefit from different types of food. For example, dogs that shed need different amounts of amino acids in their food than dogs that do not shed. Heavy dogs need different amounts of minerals in their food than lighter dogs, as their bones have different nutritional requirements. Some brands have different products for different breeds. You can also research the foods that are best for your breed on your own, as there are many articles published for the concerned dog owner.

6 **Allergies** You might notice that your dog is allergic to some foods. Pay attention to the ingredients in the foods he has problems with, and try different foods with different ingredients. Common ingredients that dogs are allergic to include beef, chicken and chicken products, wheat, dairy, corn and soy. Try eliminating one of these at a time from your dog's diet to determine which one is causing the problem. If your dog is still having issues with allergies, consult your vet.

76

7 **Health problems** Some breeds are prone to certain ailments, some of which can be mitigated by giving them food with supplements and extra nutrients in it. For example, if your dog has Cushing's disease (a condition that results from the chronic overproduction of too much glucocorticoid), he will be healthier on a diet high in protein and low in fat, fiber and purine (an excess of uric acid that can precipitate gout attacks). If your dog has a health problem, ask your vet for advice on what your dog should be getting in his food.

8 **Supplements** Choosing a dog supplement is often dictated by shortcomings the dog owner is trying to address. Some people add Vaseline to their dog's food to improve the shininess of its coat. Older dogs may require an enzyme supplement to help them digest their food. Some supplements can help ease arthritis pains.

9 **Budget** While you may be willing to spend whatever it takes to get the perfect dog food, you may not be able to afford your top choice. At the same time, you should not let price be your only factor when choosing your dog's food, as this is a big influence on his health. If you cannot afford to buy "all natural" dog foods, you might be able to afford to buy cheap meat intended for humans. Cook it for your dog and serve it with vegetables.

10 **Your dog's preferences** Finally, don't forget to consider what your dog prefers. Picking out the perfect food won't do any good if your dog refuses to eat it. On the other hand, you can make a healthy food more tempting by adding bits of meat or soup stock for flavoring, so don't give up right away if he refuses your food choices.

5 Key Dog Food Ingredients

Making sure your dog is fed high-quality food is essential for her health and happiness. There are dozens of dog food brands to choose from, some offering more nutritional value than others. Many dog owners prefer to make their own pet food so they have more control over the ingredients in each meal. Whatever you decide to do, here are the five key dog food ingredients that your pet's food should contain:

1 **Chicken or fish** These are the best sources of protein for most dogs. Dogs need ample amounts of protein in each meal to stay strong and maintain a healthy coat. In fact, they need 22 amino acids to stay healthy, and 10 of them must be obtained from food. Just keep in mind that a higher percentage of protein listed on the package doesn't necessarily make it better. The protein needs to come from a real source such as real chicken or fish meat in order to provide any nutritive value to your pet.

2 **Brown rice** This is a healthy source of carbohydrates that your dog needs for energy. Many dry pet food formulas are made with brown rice. The extra fiber is what makes this a healthier choice over white rice for your dog. Many dogs can also tolerate brown rice better than foods made with white rice because it's easy to digest and typically does not cause constipation.

3 **Fatty acids** Essential fatty acids are important for a shiny coat, healthy eyes and strong muscles. Your dog can benefit from both omega-3 and omega-6 fatty acids; pet food manufacturers may have this ingredient listed as an additive. Any animal or plant sources of this oil are ideal. Look for chicken fat, canola oil or herring oil on the ingredients list.

4 **Eggs** These are another great source of protein for your dog, and are often found as a main ingredient in some of the best brands. Eggs contain protein and several vitamins including vitamin B, E and K.

5 **Corn gluten** This is often used as a filler ingredient in lower-quality pet food, but it can be acceptable if it is used in a small amount to complement real meat and brown rice in the product. Corn gluten is a source of carbohydrate that can provide energy for your active dog.

Finding the best dog food for your puppy or mature dog can take time, but your efforts will pay off. A dog that is fed high-quality foods is likely to stay happy, healthy and strong for years to come.

Choosing a Dog Food: Does Kibble Size Matter?

A visit to the grocery or pet store can be overwhelming. There are dozens of different brands of dog food, and each seems to offer dozens of choices. Do you want wet or dry? Chunky or smooth? Chicken or beef flavor? Or perhaps seafood? Even worse, there are different sizes of kibble for different dogs. Choosing the right one can be tricky, which is why we've rounded up the below tips on picking the right food for your canine.

- **Small dogs** Generally, dog food size is proportionate to the size of the animal. Smaller dogs need smaller pieces to chew and digest properly. If you give small animals pellets that are too small, they might choke on each morsel as they try to bolt it down. However, this can vary from one canine to another. In most cases, food for pooches under 25 pounds should be about half the size of a kernel of corn. When you pour it into the bowl, it might seem as though you are feeding your dog too much because pellets this size tend to clump together. However, you should be safe following the guidelines on the back of the bag.

- **Large dogs** Large animals are a different story. Their jaws are more powerful and they are able to swallow larger pieces of food without causing digestive distress or clogs in the back of the throat. Kibble for dogs over 50 pounds is often the size of a penny in diameter, though slightly smaller bits are usually not dangerous. As large dogs get older, it might be necessary to purchase food that is smaller. Their teeth become brittle and they might have difficulty swallowing large pieces, so pay attention to how long it takes your dog to eat and make adjustments as necessary.

- **Medium dogs** If your dog falls somewhere in the middle, you'll need to find a middle-grade kibble to feed him. It might be necessary to try several different brands and sizes until you find one that he prefers, but don't stress too much over whether the pellets are too large. Young dogs can crunch their kibble into smaller pieces, and are surprisingly adept at making their own adjustments.

- **Dogs that bolt** Some dogs have trouble eating dry food because they eat too fast, bolting down the pellets without chewing them. This can lead to stomachaches, ulcers and even ruptures in the stomach, and cause constipation if it happens on a regular basis. If your pooch tends to bolt his dog food, you can mix dry with wet food, or wet the kibble before giving it to him. This will soften the pellets and make it easier for him to digest his meal, even if he does tend to wolf it down.

Many dog owners agonize about the right type of food to buy, but there is very little on the market that will cause your pet harm in the short term. If you're having trouble finding a happy medium, or if your dog changes his eating habits suddenly, ask your veterinarian for advice right away.

Pet Care 101: Wet vs. Dry Dog Food

For dog owners who like to pamper their pets, feeding only kibble to a dog may seem like culinary torture. However, for the average dog, dry dog food is a healthy and budget-conscious choice.

Dog owners who feed their pets dry food are promoting overall dental health and preventing canine cavities. In addition to brushing a dog's teeth, a dog owner can feed dry food to a pooch to help remove tartar from its teeth.

Veterinarians also recommend dry food to help puppies develop healthy jaw strength. Dry food is ideal for the dog who does not like chew toys, and it trains pets to slow down and chew their dinner properly.

Dry food has many other advantages over wet food. In addition to being easier to store and transport, dry food is less difficult to measure, which increases pet owners' ability to feed dogs the right portions. It also is cost-effective, and dog owners often pay less for premium dry food than wet food.

However, wet food is a good option for dogs with reduced jaw strength or those with preexisting dental problems who are unable to properly chew dry dog food. A veterinarian also may prescribe wet food for short periods of time to settle digestive problems or help a dog gain weight.

If you've already started your dog on wet food but would like to make the switch to dry, talk to your veterinarian. Most veterinarians can recommend a dry food that will meet the nutritional needs of your dog. A veterinarian also may want to monitor your dog's weight to ensure he does not lose significant weight during the transition from wet to dry food.

Most dogs will change to dry food with little fuss, but there are a few tricks to make the process easier. Expect a two-week transition from wet to dry food. Start by feeding your dog one-fourth dry dog food and the remaining amount of the meal in wet food. This should help you avoid any digestive problems. Mixing a little warm water with the food also should help during the initial adjustment.

5 Reasons to Switch to Organic Dog Food

Just as you wouldn't knowingly eat food that has been sprayed with harmful pesticides and herbicides, you would not expose your dog to those same hazardous chemicals in its meals. For many dog owners, organic dog food offers a safe, nutrient-rich alternative to cheaply made foods containing artificial pesticides, hormones, fillers and preservatives. Here are five reasons to feed your pooch organic food.

1 **Feed your dog a nutritionally balanced meal.** Organic pet food generally is more wholesome. Some nature-based brands promote grain-free diets. Others offer holistic dog food that provides a good balance of dogs' nutritional needs. Many lower-cost, name-brand selections, including veterinarian-recommended meals, contain substandard fillers and animal byproducts that offer pets little nourishment.

2 **Promote a healthier lifestyle.** Producing organic food incorporates good farming practices, and this in turn ensures your dog receives a toxin-free diet. By presenting your dog with healthy food, you may be helping to extend and improve the quality of its life. Organic pet food contains all-natural ingredients, so you can rest assured your dog will not be harmed by harmful, low-quality byproducts.

3 **Improve digestive function.** If your dog has a sensitive stomach and vomits regularly, chemically treated grains within your dog's food may be to blame. Organic food, on the other hand, has all-natural ingredients that foster proper digestive health. While nonorganic meals are less expensive than their organic counterparts, consider that you are paying less for low-quality, byproduct-filled food that may harm your pet. Organic foods also promote a more bio-original diet, focusing on protein that dogs need.

4 **Foster healthy hair and skin.** Some dog owners say organic food improved the softness and luster of their dogs' coats. One explanation for this is the rich vitamin and mineral content of organic food. Healthier hair prevents excessive shedding. Organic food can add to your dog's well-being by blocking its susceptibility to skin-and-coat irritants. Natural food, grown free of artificial chemicals and additives, also provides more essential amino acids, used to develop healthy fur.

5 **Reduce allergies.** Some dogs have allergic reactions to products within their food. Organic dog food prevents dogs' exposure to allergens that may have been introduced into pet food through additives. It also provides your dog a balanced diet, the lack of which could cause allergies.

5 Reasons to Make Your Own Dog Food

Your dog needs a balanced diet to stay healthy and strong. Yet feeding your pets commercial, processed foods and snacks can make their meals less than nutritious. Many pet foods contain additives and filler ingredients that do not provide any nutritional value, and can even make your dog sick. You can provide better nutrition for your dog by making your own dog food using some simple ingredients and cooking techniques. Here are just five reasons why pet owners should make their own dog food.

1 **Avoid pet food recalls.** Dozens of major pet food brands have issued recalls, which means you always need to be vigilant about the brands you choose, which may lead to changing your dog's regular diet. Most dogs do well with a simple and consistent diet, so changing brands regularly can be detrimental to their health. Plus, you may have to deal with the side effects of contaminated foods when you only feed your pet commercially prepared food.

2 **Reduce the risk of allergies.** Many commercially prepared foods contain chemicals, additives and even some foods that can trigger an allergic reaction or cause a food intolerance. Animal byproducts and some whole grains can be indigestible. When you make your own dog food, you can use only the most nutritious and wholesome ingredients.

3 **Supply only fresh, healthy ingredients.** When you're in control of the food-making process, you get to choose the ingredients. Recommended foods include cooked brown rice, boiled vegetables, cooked ground beef and boiled chicken or turkey. There are hundreds of different homemade pet food recipes available. In most cases, you can refrigerate unused portions for up to three days, so your dog will always be fed fresh food at every meal.

4 **Reduce the risk of bloating and indigestion.** Many dogs experience bloating, indigestion or even diarrhea after eating certain types of store-bought foods. Holistic veterinarians say that many commercial foods (even premium brands) are made with fillers that absorb a lot of water in the stomach. This causes excessive bloating and discomfort, and can take its toll on your pet's health.

5 **Improve your dog's health.** If you feed your dog an all-natural diet, you may notice her coat become silkier, her eyes brighter, and her energy increase. Some experts also recommend the biologically appropriate raw food or Bones and Raw Food (BaRF) diet for domestic canines, where nothing is cooked. The premise of this diet is to go back to the wild ancestry of dogs and feed a diet that is not processed or cooked. Meals are comprised of bones with meat attached, organs, muscle, eggs, fruit, vegetables, whole-grain cereals and some supplements.

There are several nutritional benefits to feeding your dog homemade meals, but it can take time for her to adjust. You may need to use dietary supplements to make sure your dog is getting the proper nutrients at each meal, but homemade pet food is still a much healthier alternative to store-bought varieties. Research some recipes and check in with your veterinarian if you're planning on making the shift to homemade meals for your dogs and puppies.

82

5 Dog Food Ingredients to Avoid

While many people can read nutrition labels for their families, understanding dog food labeling and ingredients still presents a challenge. Although you should talk with your veterinarian and use your discretion when choosing food, these five ingredients never should be in food you feed your pet.

1 **Digest** Digest is a general term for parts of animal tissue. Although regulations specify that no feathers, teeth, horns or hair should be present in the food, digest contains almost every other part of an animal. These parts are cooked into a broth that is then added to food as a flavor enhancer. While some digests are identified as specific types of meat, others generally are labeled "digest." This labeling gives dog food manufacturers flexibility to include more animals in the food, such as roadkill, euthanized shelter animals and animals that were ill or died from an illness before they were slaughtered.

2 **Chicken byproduct meal** Chicken byproduct meal contains chicken parts unfit for your dog's regular consumption. This includes necks, feet and organs. These chicken byproducts may add flavor and protein, but they are more difficult to digest than chicken meat. Look for chicken meat instead of chicken meal or chicken byproducts when picking food.

3 **Salt** Too much salt intake is as unhealthy for animals as it is for humans. Salt, often listed as sodium chloride on food labels, is a flavor enhancer that should be minimized in your pet's diet. While pet foods generally contain sufficient amounts of salt, it often is overused in poor-quality foods to add flavor and make the food more interesting.

4 **Corn syrup** Corn syrup also is used as a flavor enhancer. However, there is no need for such additives, especially if the food is made with quality ingredients. Like humans, dogs that consume too many sweets can be at greater risk for hypoglycemia, tooth decay and obesity. Dogs also can become addicted to sugar, making it difficult to switch to a healthier food.

5 **Peanut hulls** Peanut hulls are included in inexpensive dog foods to add bulk. These hulls offer no nutritional value—not even usable fiber. Additionally, pesticide residue may be on the hulls.

10 Toxic Foods for Dogs

By making sure that you know about the most toxic foods for your dog, you can ensure that your pet stays healthy and avoids unneeded trauma or health issues. The following are 10 common household foods that are extremely toxic to dogs.

1 **Chocolate, coffee, tea, soda and anything else containing caffeine** These items all have compounds that are known to be toxic to dogs, causing severe heart and nervous system damage. Be very careful not to let dogs get even a bit of these things, be they in icing, cocoa powder or even chocolate milk. The quantity needed to affect a dog varies with body mass, but avoid them at all costs.

2 **Bones from fish, poultry and other meat sources** If not chewed properly, they can cause obstruction or laceration of the digestive system.

3 **Onions and garlic** These can cause severe liver damage and can be fatal in certain quantities. Make sure that you prevent your dog from having any kind of onion, be it dried, shredded or of any color. Watch out for garlic and garlic oil or powder, which can be found on bread and other commonly eaten prepared foods.

4 **Nuts** Most nuts are bad for dogs; macadamia nuts are the worst. Nuts have compounds that accelerate the growth of bladder stones and weaken the bones.

5 **Avocado and persimmons** Avocados cause fluid accumulation in the lungs and are very toxic to dogs. Every part of them, including fruit, pits, skin and leaves, are dangerous. The same goes for persimmons.

6 **Tomatoes, potatoes and rhubarb** Tomatoes, especially unripe green ones, are toxic and can cause all sorts of problems that can lead to heart failure. Potato skins are especially bad for dogs, as is the entire rhubarb plant. In fact, some parts of rhubarb are toxic to humans, too.

7 **Grapes and raisins** An unknown toxin can damage the kidneys. There have been no problems associated with grape seed extract.

8 **Nutmeg** This appears in various foods, especially those eaten around the holidays. It can be lethal to dogs. Avoid feeding gingerbread cookies, eggnog and other nutmeg-laced products to your canine friend.

9 **Alcohol** While it is something that may happen in movies and on television, dogs should never ingest liquor of any sort in real life. Alcohol causes various behavioral problems (similar to humans) and may cause seizures, cardiac arrest, coma and death, depending on how much alcohol a dog has consumed.

10 **Baking soda, baking powder and yeast** Leavening agents can cause serious problems for dogs, including spasms, seizures and heart problems. Effects may not be noticed immediately, so make sure you get your dog to the vet quickly.

Choosing a Dog Food for Pets with Allergies

Food allergies account for almost 10 percent of the allergies a dog can experience; many pet owners don't realize that dog food is the culprit. You will know when your dog is experiencing a food allergy because she will start scratching, become irritable, and her skin will turn red or break out in hives or sores.

Many processed and packaged foods can trigger an allergic reaction; the biggest offenders are some of the most common ingredients found in major pet foods. Wheat, corn and even chicken can be the reason your dog is experiencing an allergic reaction. Here are some tips for choosing the best dog food for a pet with allergies:

- **Choose a protein your dog doesn't usually eat.** Most pet food for dogs is made with chicken or beef, but your dog may be allergic to either of these protein sources. Consider feeding her food made with lamb; it's considered to be an all-purpose protein and typically does not trigger an allergic reaction.

- **Steer clear of dairy products.** Many dogs cannot tolerate dairy very well. Read the ingredients of all packaged foods to make sure there are no dairy products or dairy derivatives present in the formula.

- **Provide food that contains enough healthy fats.** Excessive scratching and itching can be a sign of inflammation, which is linked to a lack of omega-3 and omega-6 in the diet. Make sure the food is either a natural source of these fats, or consider adding a food additive to meals as a supplement.

- **Switch to a grain-free diet.** Many processed foods are made with wheat and whole-grain filler ingredients. Unfortunately, these can be the source of an allergic reaction. Look for natural, organic blends that are made only with pure ingredients and do not contain any type of wheat or grains. You can reintroduce healthier grains such as oatmeal or barley only when you've ruled out the possibility that your dog is allergic to these foods.

- **Stick with all-natural and organic processed foods.** If you are feeding your pet processed foods, make sure the food does not contain animal byproducts or additives. While these can help the food last longer, they can compromise the health of your pet. All-natural and organic products will be assimilated better, provide better nutrition and have little or no risk of triggering an allergic reaction.

Choosing the right dog food for a pet with allergies can be a complicated process because every dog's needs are different, but you can keep your pet happy and healthy with a little planning and research. Use some of these strategies when shopping for pet food so your dog can get the essential nutrition she needs without compromising her health and well-being.

Choosing the Right Dog Food for Senior Pets

Mature dogs have very different nutritional requirements from puppies and active adult dogs, which is why many dog food brands offer a special line of food that contains fewer calories and protein than conventional formulations. It's important to cut down on the quantity of food at each meal for dogs that are older because they may not be as active, and their bodies will need to work harder to digest large amounts of food. Older dogs may also need to take supplements to balance out their diet and protect their bones and joints. Here are some tips for choosing the right dog food for your older dog:

- **Make sure the dog food contains quality protein.** Read the ingredients carefully to make sure the first five to seven ingredients contain sources of real fish, chicken, beef or eggs. Meat byproducts may not provide the same nutritional value and can be difficult to digest. If your dog isn't able to digest her food completely, she may be at risk for nutritional deficiencies.

- **Make sure the brand has been evaluated by the AAFCO.** The Association of American Feed Control Officials profiles and reviews different types of pet food on the market, giving those that qualify an official stamp of approval. An AAFCO stamp ensures that the food has met its strict standards.

- **Review calorie requirements.** Check with your vet to determine how many calories your mature dog really needs, and make sure you're staying within the appropriate range when selecting foods and snacks. Many pet owners make the mistake of overfeeding their dogs because they are not paying attention to the dog's daily caloric intake. Remember that older dogs need far fewer calories than adult dogs and puppies because they are less active and have stopped growing.

- **Steer clear of filler ingredients.** Many types of pet food are made with filler ingredients such as corn gluten or wheat products that add bulk and weight to the food. The extra fiber and bulk can be too difficult to process and digest for your senior pet, so they may not be able to meet her daily dietary needs. Look for organic, mildly processed foods, or consider making your own food so that your dog is always eating a high-quality meal.

- **Stick with soft and "wet" foods.** Some senior dogs suffer from dental problems and can have difficulty chewing on bones and certain types of dry food. Stick with wet foods and softer varieties that will be easy to break down in the mouth and stomach.

Senior dogs have some very special dietary needs because of decreased activity levels and declining health. Make sure you check with your vet before making any drastic changes to your pet's diet, and pay attention to pet food labels so you can find the best match for your dog.

Choosing a Dog Food for an Overweight Dog

A few extra treats a day or some careless food measuring can lead to your dog packing on the pounds. While additional exercise and portion control can help your dog lose the weight, many choose to feed their dog a diet dog food to encourage timely weight loss. These foods are specially formulated to provide a feeling of fullness without the calories of a normal dog food.

Before shopping Before choosing a dog food, talk to your veterinarian. Most veterinarians know that obesity in dogs can lead to health complications, especially for certain breeds. This will make your vet your dog's greatest advocate for losing weight. A veterinarian should weigh your dog and determine what is a reasonable weight, as well as the minimum food your dog should receive. For weight loss of more than a few pounds, a time frame for weight loss should also be discussed. If weight loss is stubborn with portion control and regular exercise, a veterinarian may prescribe a dog food. These prescription foods are held to strict dietary standards to promote healthy, reasonable weight loss. However, their high price tag often makes them a last resort for dog owners.

Reading the labels Just like shopping at the grocery store, choosing a dog food for your dog's weight loss is all about proper nutrition. Ask your veterinarian for percentages of protein and fat each food should contain. Veterinarians often recommend low-carbohydrate, high-protein food for dogs. You should ideally avoid high percentages of bulking agents such as corn and wheat. Many dog foods offer weight-control formulas that may help your dog with the transition and portion control. These dog foods often contain large amounts of fiber, which reduces the need to drastically cut portion sizes. Keep in mind that you should be feeding your dog for his ideal weight, not his current weight. Also, always feed him twice a day to prevent low blood sugar.

How to Exercise Your Dog

Your dog needs a minimum of 20 minutes of exercise daily to stay healthy.

You may break a sweat, but you won't have to work like a dog to get your pooch panting. A walk around the neighborhood, a romp at a local park or a short hike in the woods is great exercise. Throw a tennis ball for a game of fetch, let him swim in a lake or pool, or take him to an off-leash dog park so he can run around with other dogs. Changing your route or walking at different times of the day will keep your pet's interest and energy levels up. Carry water with you and don't overwork your dog when it's hot.

Although weight-control food is often available in both wet and dry varieties, stick to the kibble if possible when choosing a dog food. Wet food can often cause dental problems. Dry kibble, on the other hand, will help remove tartar and keep teeth in good condition. Owners of dogs that have existing dental problems and that regularly eat wet food should consult a veterinarian before making any changes.

Puppy Health 101: Get the Answers to All the Important Questions

Pet health determines the quality of your pet's life, so it's vital to start caring for your puppy's health from Day One. Here are some common questions about caring for your puppy.

When do I begin vaccinations?

Within the first 17 weeks of her life, a puppy needs to receive several vaccinations. They must occur repeatedly every three to four weeks. Without them, a young pup can suffer from common canine ailments such as distemper. Check with your veterinarian regularly to determine the proper schedule for vaccinations.

When should I spay or neuter my puppy?

Spay or neuter your puppy within the first six months of his or her life. These procedures are vital to pet health and quality of life. For females, spaying helps them avoid certain diseases such as mammary cancer. With males, neutering decreases their level of aggression. Spaying and neutering also helps control pet population, which reduces the number of strays and disease.

What kinds of ailments should I be watching out for?

Puppies can fall prey to skin infections. As a result, you must inspect their skin regularly. Check for thinning hair, bumps and skin discoloration. If you see an infection, keep the area clean until you can get her to a vet. You may have to apply an ointment or give your puppy oral antibiotics.

How important is exercise for a puppy?

Obesity is a growing problem for today's dogs. So, start your puppy on an exercise routine that includes a vigorous two-block walk. This type of exercise will strengthen her heart and the rest of her body, too. Also be sure to complement your dog's exercise routine with a healthy, lean diet. Check dog food labels and make sure the contents are made with meat. Also, don't overfeed your puppy, even if she begs you for more.

How much grooming is necessary for my puppy?

Pet grooming and pet health go hand in hand. Brush your puppy's coat and teeth daily to reduce the chances of skin and gum disease. Also, manicured nails will help your puppy's gait and paw development. Finally, be sure to bathe your dog regularly with a natural anti-flea shampoo.

Do I have to "puppy-proof" my house?

Electrical cords, socks, garbage and small dog toys are all hazards for puppies. They can chew or swallow them and choke. So, it's up to you to keep them away from her. If this isn't possible, mark off a safe area in the house for your puppy to play and reduce her chances of hurting herself by keeping doors to unsafe areas closed.

5 Common Pet Health Problems for Puppies

Puppies are energetic, lively little animals that need constant attention and good nutrition to grow into healthy dogs. Unfortunately, many are prone to getting sick, especially during their weaning months. If left untreated, a simple pet health problem can turn into something much more serious. Keep an eye peeled for the warning signs and symptoms to make sure your little friend stays healthy and happy. Here are just five common pet health problems that puppies of all types can experience.

1 **Cough** A hacking cough is typically caused by a bacterial or viral infection, and can be picked up from virtually anywhere. Your puppy may be on the verge of developing this problem if you notice she's not barking properly and seems to be ill tempered. A dry cough can be treated with medication or herbal remedies; just head to the vet for a recommended treatment plan.

2 **Scabies** Sarcoptic mange, also known as scabies, is quite common in young pups of all breeds. The skin condition can make your puppy very agitated and irritated. You'll know your puppy has it when she can't stop scratching herself. But be warned, this condition is contagious. If you think your puppy has scabies, you will need to head to the vet immediately for treatment.

3 **Diarrhea** This is common in newborn puppies that are just starting to eat solid foods. However, it can also be an indication of an illness or disease, so it's important to take your puppy to the vet as soon as you notice that her feces aren't looking healthy. Puppies can get diarrhea from eating contaminated food, eating other dogs' feces, or simply because of a viral infection. It's best to get them to the vet ASAP for a checkup.

4 **Vomiting** Some puppies can vomit when they become overly anxious or excited, if they start running around after eating, or if they eat too fast. Make sure your puppy isn't being overfed at each meal, and deliver her meal in a calm and peaceful setting so she's not stressed out by her environment. If vomiting continues for more than 24 hours, it's time to see the vet.

5 **Parvo** This can affect many puppies who are still being weaned. Parvo is a very contagious disease that can cause severe intestinal and cardiac problems. Signs of parvo include extreme lethargy, loss of appetite, difficulty sleeping, general agitation and fever. If you detect any of these signs, it's important to see the vet immediately. Parvo can be fatal if left untreated.

Many pet health problems that affect puppies can be handled with early detection and preventive measures. Make sure your puppy has had all of her vaccinations. Keep an eye on her for any symptoms of the five ailments above so your puppy stays happy, strong and healthy for years to come.

Pet Care Basics: How to Choose a Veterinarian

If you're like most Americans, at some time in your life you've moved to a new town and had to choose a new family doctor. It's the same for your pets, except for one major difference: You're the one who decides if the veterinarian is a good match for your pet. Don't take choosing a veterinarian lightly; your pet's health and well-being depend on your choice. And remember: The best pet care is preventive pet care, so once you've chosen a veterinarian, be sure to return regularly for annual checkups.

Here are some tips on how to choose the best veterinarian for your pet:

- **Start your search for a veterinarian before you need one.** It's better to invest the time and find a good vet before your pet gets sick, so you don't have to start looking for a vet when you're scared and under pressure.

- **Ask friends, coworkers or relatives to recommend a veterinarian.** Ask why they like that particular vet. Is he or she gentle with the animals? Affordable? Does the vet help you make decisions and give you options rather than telling you what you must do?

- **Check your town's Yellow Pages for vets nearby.** This can be a good place to start. There are also many online sources that can help you locate a veterinarian. One is LocalVets.com. Also call your state veterinary medical association for specialist referrals in your area.

- **Drop by the vet's office to make an appointment.** See how you feel in the waiting room. If the vet's office is really posh, consider that you'll be paying higher fees for your pet care than if the office is nice and simple. Also take into account how easy or difficult it will be to get to the veterinarian. Ask about the office's regular hours and emergency care after hours and on weekends and holidays.

- **See how you feel about the reception staff.** Are they willing to answer your questions? Do they seem to know what they're talking about? And most important, do they seem to like animals? If you have a good feeling about the office, make an appointment for your dog. It's fine to start with a brief checkup, just to establish a relationship with the veterinarian and to ask any questions about your pet's needs. When you meet the vet, make sure you and your pet feel comfortable. If not, keep looking. No one says you have to stay with the first one you meet.

10 Essential Pet First Aid Kit Items

Pets catch spring fever, too; they can hardly wait to soak up the sunshine and warm breezes with you. But with their increased outdoor exposure comes an additional risk for injuries and accidents. So what's a concerned pet owner to do? Enjoy the season, but be vigilant about your pet's health by putting together a first aid kit in a waterproof box for warm-weather emergencies.

The essential element of any first aid kit is a list of emergency phone numbers that includes your veterinarian, an after-hours emergency veterinary hospital and the ASPCA's Animal Poison Control Center (888-426-4435). The last thing you want to do in an emergency is hunt around for 10 minutes looking for these very important phone numbers. Tape the phone list to the inside of the box. Then, be sure to include these key items on the inside:

1 **Muzzle** This item is a must for preventing your pet from defensively biting you while you attend to the injury. Even the sweetest of our furry friends can bite when frightened or in pain.

2 **E-collar** (Elizabethan collar) A plastic cone (think: inverted lampshade) that attaches around the pet's neck, the E-collar is key in keeping pets from doing more harm to their injuries, such as licking their wounds, which can introduce harmful bacteria to an open sore. There's nothing owners hate more than the E-collar. Although silly-looking, it's a necessary evil.

3 **Digital thermometer** Sold at any drugstore, a thermometer is key in gauging how sick your pet really is. The average temperature range for a dog is 100°F to 102.5°F. A temperature lower than 100 or higher than 104 is an emergency that requires immediate attention from a vet.

4 **Hydrogen peroxide** This household item is useful in cleaning wounds, but also for inducing vomiting if a pet has swallowed something dangerous. Always check with your veterinarian or the Poison Control Center before inducing vomiting, because if the substance ingested is caustic, it might be more harmful coming back up.

5 **Triple antibiotic ointment** This is good for keeping small wounds and lacerations free of infection. It can often be more effective than taking antibiotics by mouth.

6 **Styptic powder** This helps stop the bleeding from a broken or torn nail, and is sold at most pet stores. You dip the nail into the powder to help form a clot. However, using household flour can also do the trick.

7 **Bandages** These include nonadhesive gauze pads, gauze rolls and flexible bandages. However, homemade pet bandages should be checked and rewrapped by a veterinarian as soon as possible after the injury. A lot more damage can be done than the initial wound if it's improperly wrapped. If you are comfortable wrapping a wound yourself, put pressure on it to help clot the bleeding, wrap it up and get your pet to a veterinarian right away.

8 **Benadryl** (diphenhydramine) To treat allergic reactions (from insect bites and bee stings), have this over-the-counter human medication on hand. It comes in a pediatric liquid variety, which allows you to give a lower dose than the adult tablets. As a rule: Give 1 to 2 mg of

Benadryl per pound of weight. For instance, if your dog weighs 5 pounds, start with 5 mg. If more is needed, increase to 10 mg.

9 Eyewash Used to flush out harmful substances sprayed into your pet's eyes, this is the same eyewash that people use, found at most drugstores. Veterinarians recommend putting an Ɛ-collar on your pet after flushing the eyes, to prevent him from scratching his cornea.

10 Tweezers These are the best tools for removing splinters and ticks. Avoid using your hands to remove a tick because of the risk of tick-borne diseases.

Remember, when dealing with any serious pet emergency, call the veterinary experts first before you head to the hospital. They can guide you through the emergency and possibly help save your dog's life before you get there.

Homegrown Healing

Sometimes you don't need to shell out for expensive prescriptions; you may have the remedy for a sick pet right at home. To be safe, call your vet to describe symptoms before you try any of these.

- **For shedding** You can add 1 or 2 tsp of peanut oil to meals, but if your pet gets loose stools, reduce the amount.

- **For general aches and pains** Dogs—not cats—can benefit from human aspirin. A 60-pound dog could take a coated adult aspirin such as Bayer with a good-size meal; a 30-pound dog could take half that much. Again, discuss this with your veterinarian.

- **For vomiting or diarrhea** Withhold food (not water) for 24 hours. You can also try Pepto-Bismol on pooches (1 tsp for a 60-pound dog, $^1/_2$ tsp for a 30-pound dog) with an OK from the doc.

- **For arthritis** People take glucosamine sulfate to increase lubrication in their joints, and dogs can, too. A 60-pound dog, for example, can be given 500 milligrams twice a day, but talk with your vet about appropriate doses.

94

5 Alternative Pet Health Remedies You've Never Heard Of

Your pet's health is always a top priority, but giving drugs or medication for health problems may not be your only option. Alternative therapies can be effective for improving the health of humans, and some believe that alternative treatments also exist for dogs. Herbal supplements and holistic treatment may be a viable solution for preventing disease, or even for treating common pet health problems.

1 **Aromatherapy to reduce aggression** If your pet becomes particularly aggressive in certain situations, a few whiffs of a calming aromatherapy treatment might help. Products such as *PetAlive.com*'s Aggression Formula promote relaxation and normal social behavior, and can help to calm down the nervous system. This can be especially effective for young puppies that get too excited when they are around children or strangers, or for older dogs that have difficulty socializing.

2 **Controlling allergies with acupuncture** This therapy has been used for thousands of years as a holistic treatment for both humans and animals in the Far East, and has only recently become a popular option in the West. Pets suffering from allergies may be able to restore their health with a series of acupuncture treatments designed to improve nervous system functionality.

3 **Probiotics or herbal parasites to improve digestion** If your dog is experiencing indigestion, constipation or other digestive problems, giving him a probiotic or healthy parasite supplement may be an effective solution. Supplements such as PetAlive's Parasite Dr. are designed to promote digestive health and balance, and to soothe the digestive system. These supplements can also serve as a tonic for the entire digestive system, so your pet is able to absorb nutrients better over time.

4 **Magnetic therapy for fatigue or depression** If your dog is experiencing a serious bout of fatigue or seems depressed, an energy-balancing treatment may help. Magnetic therapy is designed to affect the chakras in the body, and works by realigning the body's energy field. This process also increases circulation and triggers the natural healing process.

5 **Flower essences for motion sickness** Does your dog tend to get sick when you hit the road? A tincture of flower essences can be used to reduce emotional upsets associated with traveling. Liquid essences prepared from nonpoisonous flowers can help balance the mind and body, and help to improve overall health. A combination of peppermint, chamomile, meadowsweet, ginger and black horehound can help to relieve many symptoms associated with carsickness.

Pet health remedies that do not involve any drugs or synthetic chemicals may be a valuable, holistic alternative to conventional treatments. Check with your vet to see if any of these natural treatments may be an effective treatment for your dog or puppy.

All-Natural Treatments for Minor Pet Health Ailments

Pets can be rambunctious and can get into all kinds of pickles. From bee stings to minor scratches to diarrhea, it may seem like your pet invites trouble. You care about your pet's health, but you don't want to act like an overanxious parent by calling the vet every time minor ailments arise. Some education on all-natural home remedies for proper pet health is in order.

- **Treat bee stings.** After removing a bee stinger from your pet, you should prevent swelling and dull the pain. Mix 1 Tbsp baking soda with water to create a thick paste. Apply this to the infected area. You also can apply a cold ice pack to the injury.

- **Soothe mildly burned skin.** Clip most of the fur from the burned area, cleanse it with mild soap and water, and apply aloe vera to the wound. Aloe vera will soothe your pet's skin, so don't hesitate to reapply it several times throughout the day.

- **Stop diarrhea.** Pet owners hail puréed pumpkin as a great all-natural treatment for diarrhea. Your dog will love the taste of this natural healing agent.

- **Heal minor wounds.** Mixing apple cider vinegar with water will cure many small pet wounds/injuries. Simply dilute the apple cider vinegar, and apply it to your pet's wound with a clean cloth. For more serious wounds, use Dy's Liquid Bandage, which contains beeswax, herbs and olive oil.

- **Eliminate skunk odors.** When it comes to removing skunk odors, the long-discussed tomato juice remedy is, unfortunately, a myth. But there is a great all-natural treatment within your grasp. Mix water, 1 qt of hydrogen peroxide, ¼ cup of baking soda and 1 to 2 tsp of liquid soap, and apply it to your pet's fur as you would shampoo. Rinse thoroughly after several minutes. If the smell doesn't go away, feel free to reapply this solution.

While minor pet injuries often can be treated with home remedies, you should never take pet health for granted. If your pet's injury is more serious than you can safely handle, do not hesitate to call the vet immediately. Your pet's health always should be your first priority!